ALCOHOL PROBLEMS

ALCOHOL PROBLEMS

Articles published in
the *British Medical Journal*

Published by the British Medical Journal
Tavistock Square, London WC1H 9JR

ISBN 0 7279 0094 3
Made and printed in England by
The Leagrave Press Ltd, Luton and London

Preface

by the Editor
British Medical Journal

Alcohol consumption has doubled in Britain in the last 20 years, and at the same time all the measurable forms of alcohol-associated damage have also increased dramatically. The same has happened in most Western countries and in many Third World countries. Few would deny the pleasures of alcohol, and yet it may damage not only individuals but also families and whole communities in different ways. Every health and social worker—indeed, probably every individual—in Britain will be presented with some manifestation of alcohol damage. Yet at the same time as the problems have increased our thinking on alcohol has undergone a revolution.

This book, which consists of articles published in the *BMJ* and therefore held up for criticism to 95 000 readers, presents the latest thinking and information on alcohol problems. A full understanding of this multifaceted problem means considering information as diverse as the pharmacological effects of alcohol and the impact of advertising on alcohol consumption. The two parts of this book aim at providing much of what is required. The first part, by Dr Alex Paton and his colleagues, presents in a straightforward and uncomplicated way, with generous use of illustrations, what the non-specialist needs to know about understanding and managing alcohol problems, while Dr Richard Smith's more discursive part surveys current research, thinking, and controversies. (Three of these articles won Richard Smith the 1981 Periodical Publishers Association award for specialist writers.) Alcohol problems cannot be ignored, and we hope that this book provides an easy way to understanding them.

STEPHEN LOCK
1982

Contents

ABC OF ALCOHOL

ALCOHOL AND ALCOHOLISM

RICHARD SMITH

ABC OF ALCOHOL

A PATON MD, J F POTTER MB, K O LEWIS PHD
Dudley Road Hospital, Birmingham

D BISSELL
Probation Department, West Midlands

BRUCE RITSON FRCPSYCH
Alcohol Problems Clinic, Royal Edinburgh Hospital, Edinburgh

J B SAUNDERS MRCP
Liver Unit, King's College Hospital, London

G SMERDON FRCGP
Liskeard, Cornwall

DEFINITIONS

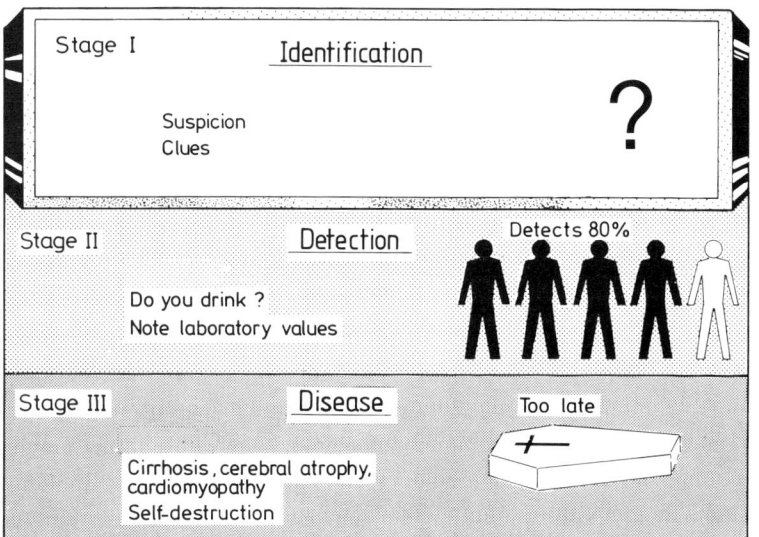

Stage I — Identification
Suspicion
Clues
?

Stage II — Detection
Do you drink?
Note laboratory values
Detects 80%

Stage III — Disease
Cirrhosis, cerebral atrophy, cardiomyopathy
Self-destruction
Too late

Confused thinking about alcohol abuse arises from (*a*) disagreement over the definition of alcoholism, (*b*) different ways of expressing alcohol consumption, and (*c*) lack of awareness, among doctors and others, of the hazards associated with excessive drinking. The purpose of these chapters is to provide background information and practical guidelines for those who are not directly concerned with alcoholism, so that they may become more sensitive to an increasingly common social phenomenon and can take action at an early stage.

No single disease

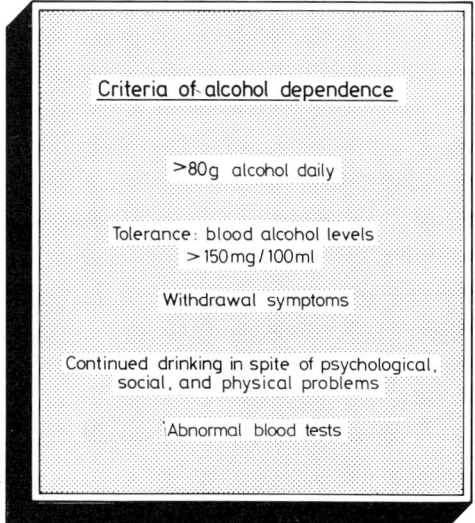

Criteria of alcohol dependence

>80g alcohol daily

Tolerance: blood alcohol levels
>150mg/100ml

Withdrawal symptoms

Continued drinking in spite of psychological, social, and physical problems

Abnormal blood tests

The term "alcoholism" is unsatisfactory because it implies a single disease. There are many different types of alcohol abuse, and a whole range of physical, psychological, and social problems is associated with excessive drinking. The term will be used here as a convenient shorthand to indicate repeated consumption of alcohol leading to dependence, physical disease, or other types of harm. In any one individual these are not necessarily directly related to the quantity of alcohol drunk, since such factors as constitution, social background, occupation, pattern of drinking, and dietary habits contribute to individual susceptibility.

A popular way of looking at alcoholism is to distinguish between alcohol-related problems and the alcohol-dependence syndrome.

A heavy drinker may or may not harm himself or others. The important thing is to recognise him and to assume that he is a potential alcoholic

Definitions

Range of drinking

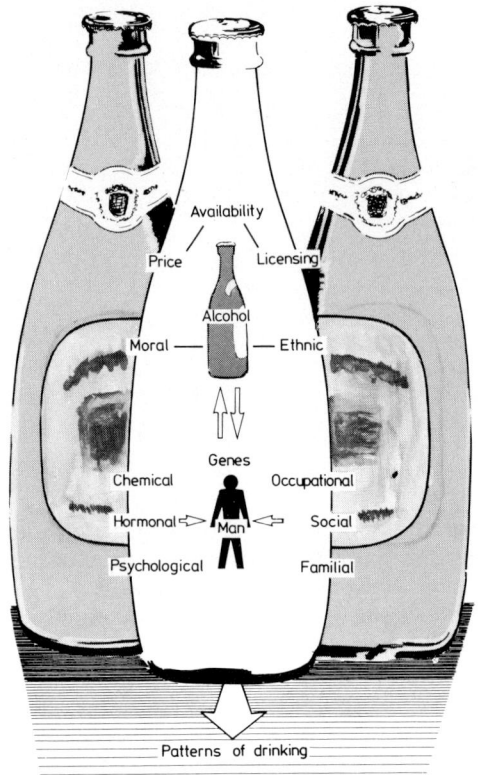

Some examples may make clear the wide range of alcoholism. A few particularly sensitive people, women more often than men, harm themselves physically from drinking "social" amounts of alcohol. They suffer from alcoholism in a medical sense, and if they could be identified they could be warned to avoid alcohol altogether.

Prolonged *heavy drinking* causes serious physical damage, such as cirrhosis, heart disease, and brain damage in about half of those who drink heavily, yet it may have no effect on the individual's personal relationships or performance at work until disease supervenes. *Problem drinkers* develop a dependence on alcohol so that they continue to drink in spite of the physical, psychological, and social problems the drinking causes. The *addicted drinker*, who has an especially high alcohol intake, seems totally unable to stop in spite of the havoc he causes, and is at risk of severe withdrawal symptoms if he does.

Skid-row alcoholics may have repeated convictions for drunkenness but in general do not develop physical disease from alcohol, perhaps because of periods of enforced abstinence which allow the body time to recover. Certain people who drink to excess may be a nuisance to themselves or others because of *personality problems* or *compulsive tendencies*, without becoming dependent on alcohol or developing physical disease.

Quantities

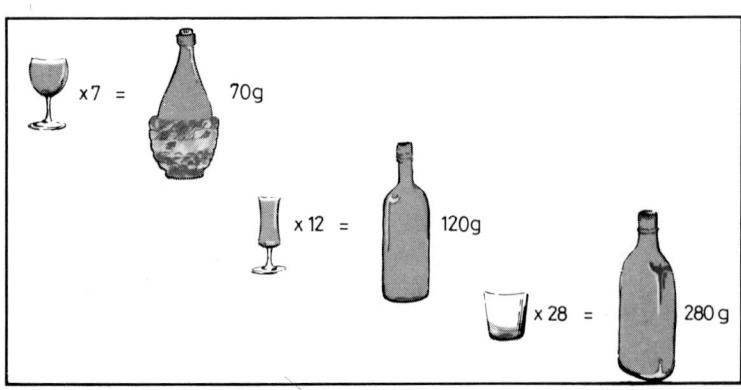

Epidemiological comparisons of alcoholism are bedevilled by lack of uniformity in designating quantities. Statements such as "five drinks a day" are meaningless, if, for example, quantity and type of alcohol are to be related to physical damage. Measurement of alcohol intake in terms of grams (g) of absolute alcohol daily is gradually being adopted for scientific and professional use. Quantities can be quickly calculated by a nomogram (see below).

One pint of beer may vary in alcohol content from 12–40 g according to strength, and one "single" of spirits, one small glass of sherry, or one glass of wine can be considered for purposes of calculation to contain 10 g (they vary from 7 to 11 g).

An agreed measure that can be readily understood by the layman is also needed. The "standard unit" used in Britain is one centilitre (again approximately 10 g) of absolute alcohol, equivalent to half a pint of average-strength beer, a "single" of spirits, a glass of wine, or a small glass of sherry.

An arbitrary level for the development of cirrhosis has been given as six pints of beer, a third of a bottle of spirits, or half a bottle of sherry daily (60–80 g alcohol), but this may be too high in some individuals. Thresholds of 120–160 g, once proposed for physical damage, are certainly excessive, and there may be no absolutely safe limits. In France, for example, thresholds as low as 60 g alcohol daily for men and 20 g for women have

Limits

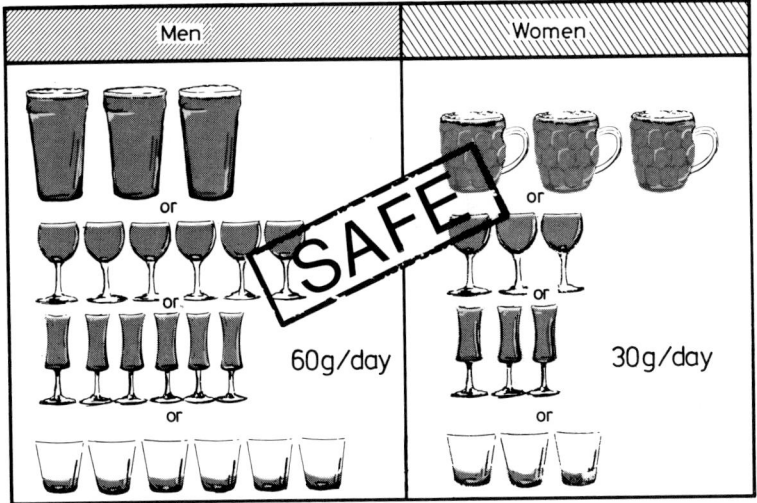

been suggested for liver damage. Men who drink more than 80 g alcohol and women who drink more than 40 g may be defined as heavy drinkers. Only the individual who is teetotal is entirely free from risk, though there is epidemiological evidence that alcohol intakes up to 30 g daily may protect against coronary artery disease.

The Royal College of Psychiatrists recommend "reasonable guidelines for the upper limit of drinking" of four pints of beer a day, four double measures of spirits, or one standard-sized bottle of wine—equivalent to about 60–80 g alcohol. There is no evidence that any one type of alcoholic drink is either more harmful or safer in its physical effects than another.

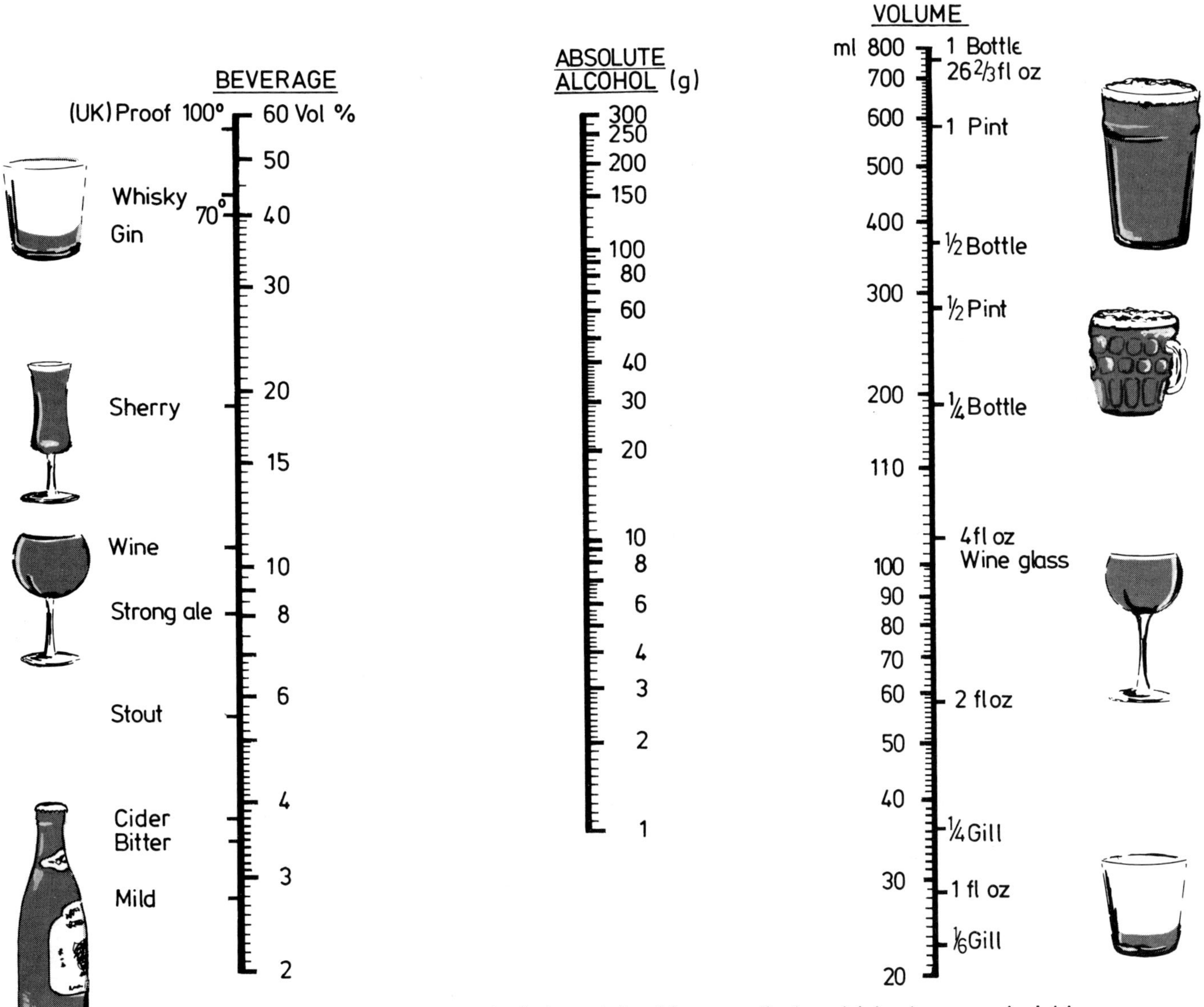

BEVERAGE

(UK) Proof 100° — 60 Vol %

Whisky 70° — 40
Gin

Sherry

Wine

Strong ale

Stout

Cider
Bitter

Mild

ABSOLUTE ALCOHOL (g)

VOLUME

ml 800 — 1 Bottle
700 — 26⅔ fl oz
600 — 1 Pint
½ Bottle
½ Pint
¼ Bottle
4 fl oz Wine glass
2 fl oz
¼ Gill
1 fl oz
⅙ Gill

To find the amount of absolute alcohol contained in a particular drink draw a straight line between the beverage and volume scales. Read the amount of alcohol in grams on the middle scale

(Mellor C S. *Br Med J* 1970; iii: 703)

NATURE OF THE PROBLEM

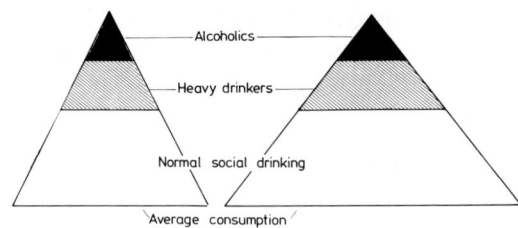

Estimates of the number of alcoholics are unsatisfactory because of lack of a suitable definition, difficulties of establishing danger levels of alcohol intake, and, above all, the formidable problems of carrying out surveys. One such survey of drinking habits, for example, uncovered less than half the known alcohol consumption. Variations in drinking patterns due to class, religion, and geographical regions are considerable.

The prevalence of alcoholism in a particular country has been related to the average alcohol intake per head: when consumption per head rises so does the number of alcohol-related problems. This is due to the shape of the distribution curve for alcohol consumption (Ledermann curve), which is continuous and skewed (log normal distribution), rather like that for blood pressure. As with the latter there is no sign of populations of "alcoholics" and "normal drinkers": a rise in overall consumption increases the number of heavy drinkers. While the Ledermann hypothesis has been disputed, it can provide an approximation of the number of people in a community drinking more than a given amount of alcohol.

For much of this century Britain has been one of the most abstemious countries in the developed world. A dramatic and continuing rise in a variety of alcohol-related problems has accompanied a steady increase in alcohol consumption per head in the past 20 years. Convictions for drunkenness currently exceed 130 000 a year, drink-driving offences total 70 000, and admissions for alcoholism to psychiatric hospitals total 20 000. The number of psychiatric admissions for alcoholism has risen 25 times in as many years and now accounts for over 10% of the total. Alcoholism causes 10 000 premature deaths a year, including its contribution to accidents and suicides.

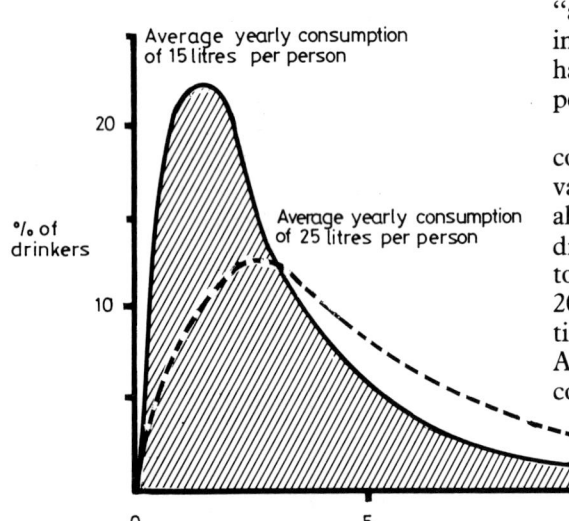

Socioeconomic influences

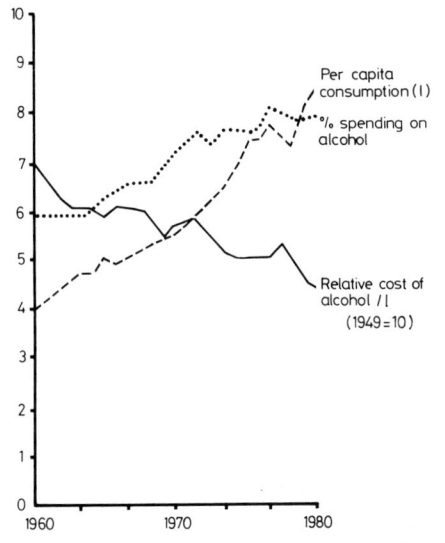

Important socioeconomic factors which lead to problem drinking are increasing unemployment, a competitive and stressful lifestyle, failure to adapt to a city environment, and depression. Increasing consumption has also been encouraged by a steady fall in the economic cost of alcohol; a higher proportion of earnings is being spent on it. Beer accounts for two-thirds of all alcohol drunk in Britain, but consumption has increased by only 45% since 1960. By contrast, drinking of wine and spirits has risen by 290% and 155% respectively, and the most striking increase has been among women.

The increase in the number of women drinkers is reflected in changes in the sex ratio of patients with alcohol-related problems. Ten years ago, for example, alcoholic cirrhosis was five times commoner in men than in women, but the male:female ratio has now fallen to 2:1. Nearly as many women as men now seek help from counselling services.

The average age at which teenagers start drinking in bars is 16 years; between 18-24 years 18% of men and 6% of women are regular heavy drinkers. Many of these subsequently reduce their intake, but physical disorders like cirrhosis may occur under the age of 30.

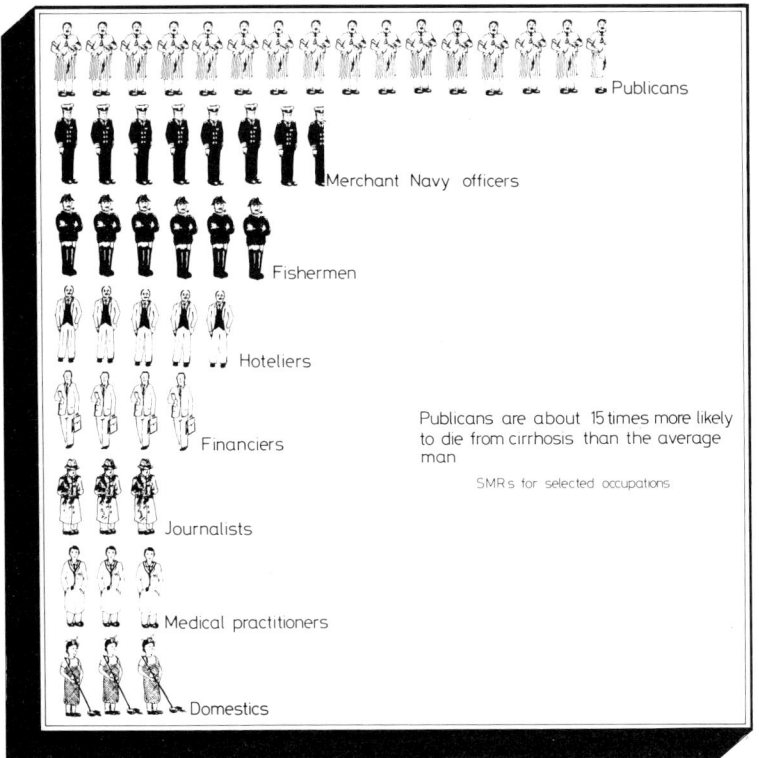

Publicans are about 15 times more likely to die from cirrhosis than the average man

SMRs for selected occupations

Occupational groups, such as business executives, members of the armed Forces and merchant navy, publicans, caterers, and hoteliers, are prone to drinking problems. The mortality rate from cirrhosis among doctors is over three times the national average. Young women in competitive careers and suburban housewives whose children have left home are also at risk.

Approximately 10% of the UK population are teetotal, while two-thirds of women and three-quarters of men drink regularly. The number of heavy drinkers (more than 80 g alcohol daily for men and more than 40 g daily for women) was estimated at two million during the 1970s, a figure which may now be out of date. About one-third of these are problem drinkers, and at least one in 10 are so *dependent on alcohol* that they suffer withdrawal symptoms when they stop drinking. For every problem drinker several members of the family suffer from the effects of his alcoholism. Relatively few alcoholics conform to the unemployed, dispossessed stereotype of the "skid row" alcoholic conspicuous in larger cities.

Some statistics

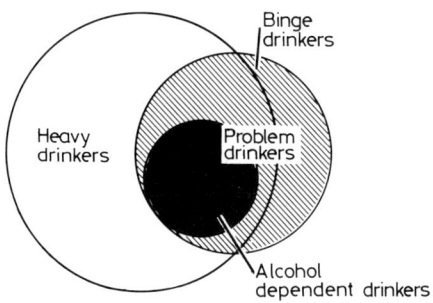

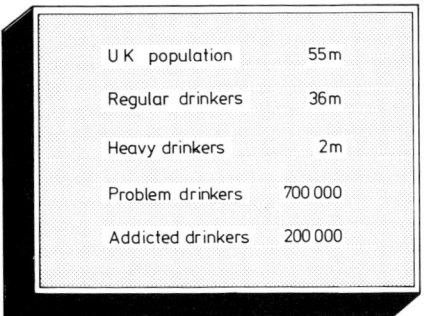

UK population	55m
Regular drinkers	36m
Heavy drinkers	2m
Problem drinkers	700 000
Addicted drinkers	200 000

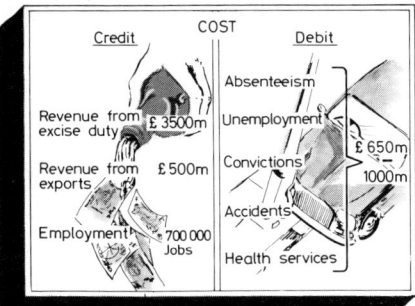

A third of patients in hospital are found to be heavy drinkers; and a third of patients attending an accident and emergency department during the evening had blood alcohol concentrations above the present legal limit of driving. While it is well known that alcohol contributes to accidents, overdoses, head injuries, and admissions for drunkenness, its more subtle effect on admissions to hospital has hardly been explored.

Up to one in five healthy men attending health screening programmes are found to have biochemical evidence of heavy alcohol consumption, though they are a selected population coming mainly from the upper social classes.

A general practitioner with 1800-1900 adults on his list will have something like 100 heavy drinkers, 40 problem drinkers, and 10 who are addicted to alcohol. Surveys suggest that only 1 in 10 heavy drinkers is known to the practice.

Many doctors and health professionals still fail to recognise the heavy drinker and even the problem drinker. Greater awareness is urgently needed: (*a*) to allow intervention at a stage when something can still be done, and (*b*) to provide better statistics.

The costs of alcoholism to the national economy are difficult to calculate, but a recent estimate put them at £1000m a year, based on costs of health care and social support for problem drinkers and their families, premature retirement, and accidents at work and on the road. This did not take into account reduced industrial efficiency and the intangible social cost of broken marriages, wife and child battering, and unemployment.

Against this might be set the £4000m revenue from duty and exports and the fact that nearly three-quarters of a million people are employed in the drinks industry; in addition 90% of drinkers enjoy alcohol without experiencing harmful effects.

Even so alcoholism cannot be viewed solely in terms of monetary costs, and most people concerned with the treatment of alcoholics believe that we have reached a stage where the social disadvantages outweigh the economic benefits.

The Ledermann curves were adapted, with permission, from an article by Dr J de Lint in *British Journal of Addiction* 1975;**70**:3-13 and the 3rd and 5th figures were reproduced by permission of the Office of Health Economics from *Alcohol: reducing the harm*, 1981.

ALCOHOL IN THE BODY

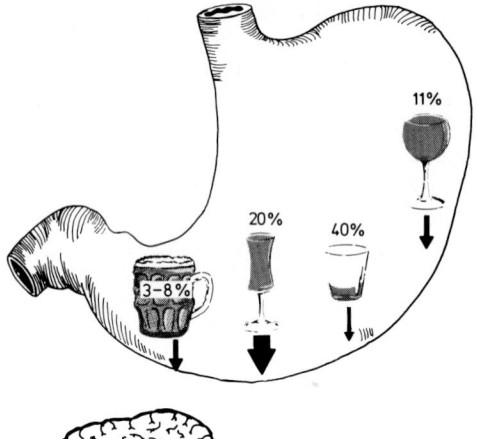

Many countries, including Britain, are suffering from an epidemic of alcoholism. Apart from the social harm, which is difficult to measure, over a hundred diseases have been attributed to alcohol abuse. It is important, therefore, that doctors know something about the handling of alcohol by the body, and some of its physiological effects.

Alcohol is absorbed from both stomach and small intestine, but is more rapidly absorbed from the latter. The rate of absorption is variable: it is most rapid when alcohol is taken on an empty stomach and when the concentration of alcohol in the drink is between 20% and 30%. Thus sherry or vermouth (approximately 20% alcohol) raise blood concentrations more rapidly than beer (3-8%), while spirits (40%) delay gastric emptying and are absorbed more rapidly when diluted. Food, and particularly carbohydrates, retards absorption considerably: blood concentrations may not reach a quarter of those in the fasted state.

Alcohol is distributed throughout the body water, so most tissues—heart, brain, and muscles—are exposed to the same concentrations as in blood. Concentrations are higher in the liver, which receives blood via the portal vein from stomach and small bowel. Little alcohol enters fat because of its poor blood supply, so that women, with more subcutaneous fat, achieve higher blood concentrations than men, even when the amount of alcohol is adjusted for body weight.

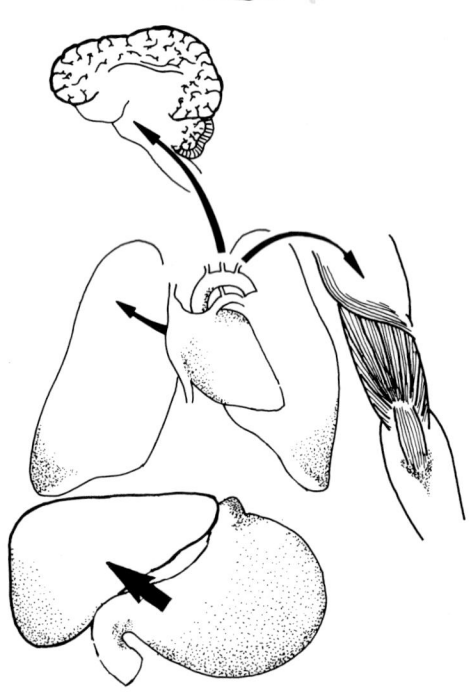

Blood alcohol concentrations vary according to sex, size, and body build, previous exposure to alcohol, type of drink, whether it is taken with food, and whether drugs that affect gastric emptying are used. Initial blood concentrations are particularly high in patients who have had a partial gastrectomy.

Alcohol is eliminated predominantly by hepatic metabolism; only 2-5% is excreted unchanged in urine or breath. The amount customarily taken by heavy drinkers represents an enormous metabolic load, and the liver's capacity for dealing with such quantities is relatively limited, although the heavy drinker may adapt for a considerable time before his liver finally fails. Half a bottle of spirits, for example, is equivalent in molar terms to 500 g of aspirin or 1·2 kg of tetracycline.

Acetaldehyde

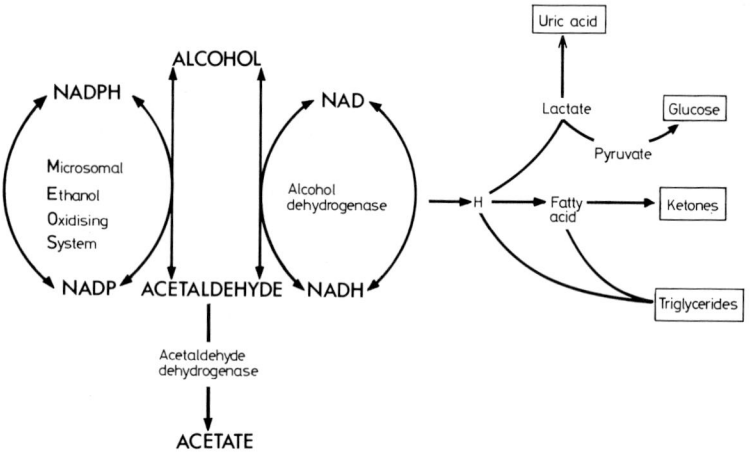

Most alcohol is metabolised to acetaldehyde, a highly reactive and toxic substance, which has been suspected for many years of being responsible for the physical damage caused by excessive alcohol consumption. Attempts to incriminate it have so far been unsuccessful. It is normally rapidly metabolised to acetate, which is not toxic, and concentrations in most tissues are extremely low.

Several metabolic abnormalities result from the oxidation of excess alcohol, including over-production of lactic and keto acids, retention of uric acid, hyperlipidaemia, and accumulation of fat in the liver.

Peak concentrations and rate of removal

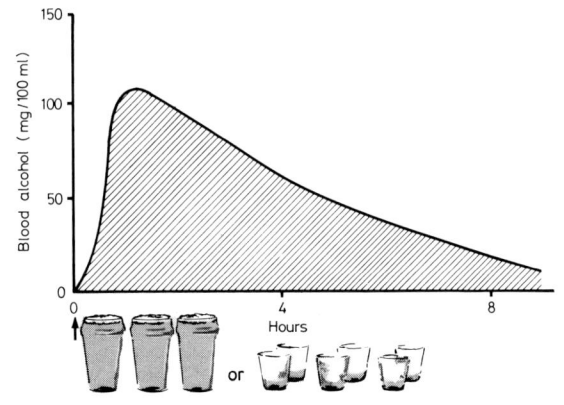

In health, alcohol is removed from the blood at a rate of about 15 mg/100 ml/h, though there is a good deal of individual variation. Metabolism is accelerated in heavy drinkers unless they have liver damage, when it may fall to less than a quarter of normal. Detectable blood concentrations are present for over eight hours after three pints of beer or three double spirits in normal people; in patients with liver damage concentrations may remain high for over 24 hours.

	Beer (pints)			Wine (glasses)			Sherry (small glasses)			Spirits (single measures)			
	1	3	5	1	3	5	1	3	5	1	2	6	12
Alcohol content (g)	20	60	100	10	30	50	10	30	50	10	20	60	120
Peak blood concentration (mg/100ml)	30	120	200	15	50	100	20	60	120	20	40	120	240

Effect on behaviour

Alcohol has a euphoriant and disinhibiting effect, but even at low blood concentrations (around 30 mg/100 ml) the risk of accidental injury increases. In a simulated driving test, bus drivers with blood alcohol concentrations of 50 mg/100 ml thought they could drive through obstacles that were too narrow for their vehicles. At 80 mg/100 ml the risk of a road accident is more than doubled; at 160 mg/100 ml it increases more than tenfold. Dysarthria and ataxia occur at concentrations of 160-200 mg/100 ml, when loss of consciousness may result. Concentrations above 400 mg/100 ml are commonly fatal, especially if a sedative drug is also taken.

30mg/100ml   50   80   120   160   200   300   400

The diagram of ethanol metabolism was adapted with permission from an article by Lieber CS. *N Engl J Med* 1978;**298**:356.

ASKING THE RIGHT QUESTIONS

Do you smoke ? What do you smoke ? How much ?

How long have you been smoking ?

Do you drink ? What do you drink ?

Roughly how much ?

How long have you been drinking ?

Do you take tablets or medicines ? What are they for ?

Many people who are not concerned with alcoholism believe that it is impossible to get reliable information about drinking patterns. The reasons given are (*a*) self-deception and guilt on the part of the alcoholic; (*b*) the difficulty in many cases of a heavy drinker, for example, a barman, being able to assess his intake; and (*c*) failure of doctors to take an adequate drinking history. Even so, 80% of alcoholics give a drinking history which tallies with that from other sources, and if quantities are accepted as approximations, valuable information can be obtained.

During history taking, questions about alcohol consumption should always be included (and recorded), both in hospital and in general practice. It is important that they be asked in the same neutral manner as other questions. They may be included with questions on symptoms or past illnesses which are relevant to the diagnosis or combined with questions on smoking and self-medication, after a review of the systems.

A positive response will allow the doctor to explore the pattern of drinking in greater detail. He can make a reasonably accurate assessment by asking what the patient has drunk in the previous week. If the answer is nothing the patient is unlikely to be an active alcoholic. If he denies drinking he should be asked why—he may abstain for religious or temperance reasons or because he is a former alcoholic.

If heavy drinking is suspected and the patient seems evasive, one technique is to use a facetious approach and to set the figure very high—for example with beer, "Thirty pints a day?"—and gradually to reduce the quantities asked. The astute observer can usually gauge the approximate level if he watches the subject's reaction. Do not be misled by the individual who says he used to drink heavily but does not do so now. Do not ask a patient whether he is an alcoholic; he will almost certainly resent the question because it conflicts with his image of himself.

Microcomputers and questionnaires

A new refinement has come with the advent of microcomputers. Programmes consisting of a series of questions on drinking habits, quantities consumed, and problems associated with heavy drinking have now been designed. They can be stored on floppy disks and used with several commercial microcomputers. The only major adaptation that needs to be made is the construction of a console (costing £100-200) by which the patient keys in his replies. This approach has been successful in obtaining reproducible histories from patients with a wide range of educational backgrounds and intelligence.

For screening patients in hospital or general practice it is appropriate to establish the pattern of drinking and average daily alcohol consumption. "Quantity-frequency" questionnaires can be used as an aide memoire; self-administered versions are particularly useful when time is at a premium. They can also be given to the spouse. Questions are asked about the type of alcohol taken, for each type the frequency of drinking using fixed-choice categories, the usual quantity on each drinking day, and the maximum amount on any one occasion. The average daily consumption can then be calculated in grams of alcohol.

A simpler method is to use a drinking diary in which the patient is asked to note down every alcoholic drink he has taken in the previous seven days. This gives a reasonable approximation to intake as established by quantity-frequency questionnaires or by interview.

Questionnaires

Several questionnaires have been developed for the diagnosis of alcoholism; the Michigan Alcoholism Screening Test (MAST) and the "CAGE" questionnaires have withstood the test of time. The MAST is available in two versions: the original 25-item questionnaire, which is administered by an interviewer, and a shorter, self-administered version comprising the 10 items of greatest discriminatory value. A score of five points or more on the Brief MAST is taken as diagnostic of alcoholism.

Both versions have been used successfully to identify alcoholics among general and psychiatric hospital patients. They are useful in screening programmes and for research, but in the clinical setting the shorter "CAGE" questionnaire, which

---

Cage

Have you ever felt you ought to *cut* down on your drinking?

Have people *annoyed* you by criticising your drinking?

Have you ever felt bad or *guilty* about your drinking?

Have you ever had a drink first thing in the morning to steady your nerves or get rid of a hangover? ("*eye-opener*")

From Mayfield D, McLeod G, Hall P. *Am J Psych* 1974;**131**: 1121-3.

Brief MAST

Circle correct answer

Do you feel you are a normal drinker? .. YES **NO (2 pts)**

Do friends or relatives think you are a normal drinker? .. .. YES **NO (2 pts)**

Have you ever attended a meeting of Alcoholics Anonymous? .. .. .. YES (5 pts) **NO**

Have you ever lost friends or girlfriends or boyfriends because of drinking? .. .. **YES (2 pts)** NO

Have you ever got into trouble at work because of drinking? .. .. .. **YES (2 pts)** NO

Have you ever neglected your obligations, your family, or your work for two or more days in a row because you were drinking? YES (2 pts) **NO**

Have you ever had delirium tremens (DTs), severe shaking, heard voices or seen things that were not there after heavy drinking? YES (5 pts) NO

Have you ever gone to anyone for help about your drinking? .. .. YES (5 pts) **NO**

Have you ever been in a hospital because of drinking? .. .. YES (5 pts) NO

Have you ever been arrested for drunken driving or driving after drinking? .. YES (2 pts) NO

Total score ....

From Pokorny AD, Miller BA, Kaplan HB. *Am J Psych* 1972;**129**:342-5.

Questionnaire for patient attending hospital or GP

Do you drink alcohol? .. .. YES NO

If NO, did you ever drink? .. .. YES NO

How old were you when you started? (Age in years) .. ..

How often do/did you drink (*Circle*)

    Daily/2-3 times a week/Once a week

    Weekends only/Once a month/Less

What do you drink? (*Circle more than one if necessary*)

    Beer—specify type (mild, bitter, lager, stout, etc) .. ..

    Spirits/Sherry/Wine/Cider

    Other—specify type (home brew, tonic wine, etc) .. ..

How much do you drink?

    Specify .... pints of beer

    .... tots/measures of spirits or part of bottle

    .... glasses of sherry, wine, cider or part of bottle

Did you use to drink more than this regularly? .. .. YES NO

Have you ever deliberately cut down on your drinking? .. YES NO

---

consists of four items, is more appropriate. Two or more positive replies are said to identify problem drinkers. Neither test should be regarded as more than 75% accurate.

Alcoholism questionnaires have the disadvantage that they depend on honest replies from an individual who may be unwilling to admit to social problems or police convictions. They lack the inherent subtlety of the medical interview, and the self-administered versions are dependent on the patient's being well enough and sufficiently motivated to complete them. By concentrating on social problems and symptoms of alcohol dependence they tend to encourage a narrow concept of alcoholism. Patients with physical diseases caused by alcohol may never have suffered any of the social consequences of heavy drinking nor been dependent on alcohol. Indeed their drinking habits may have been regarded as socially quite acceptable, so that such patients will be missed by this type of questionnaire.

The microcomputer was reproduced by permission of Commodore Ltd, Slough.

TOOLS OF DETECTION

Alcohol concentrations

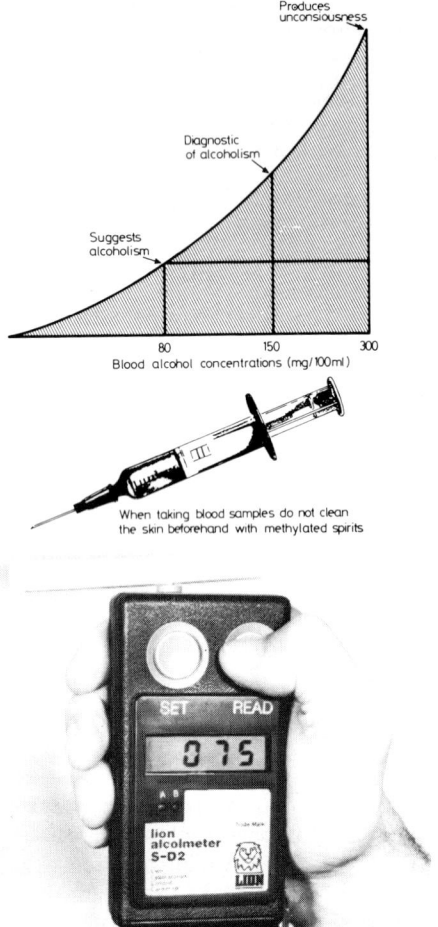

Produces
unconsciousness

Diagnostic
of alcoholism

Suggests
alcoholism

80   150   300
Blood alcohol concentrations (mg/100ml)

When taking blood samples do not clean
the skin beforehand with methylated spirits

lion
alcolmeter
S-D2

The blood alcohol concentration is not used enough as a test for alcohol abuse. It can be measured in toxicology laboratories and in many chemical pathology departments, or, if necessary, in a regional laboratory. Raised concentrations can provide incontrovertible evidence of excessive drinking, and because alcohol is eliminated relatively slowly from the blood appreciable amounts may be found for 24 hours after a drinking session.

A blood alcohol concentration exceeding 80 mg/100 ml (the legal limit for driving in Britain) is highly suggestive of alcoholism, especially in the morning, and values above 150 mg/100 ml are diagnostic. Such values do not distinguish an isolated drinking bout from chronic alcohol abuse, but if there are no signs of inebriation at concentrations of 80 mg/100 ml or more the individual may be assumed to be a heavy drinker. A blood alcohol estimation should always be considered in the unconscious patient: values usually exceed 300 mg/100 ml if alcohol is responsible.

Breath alcohol measurements reflect blood levels, are simple to perform, and provide an immediate result. Breath alcometers cost £100–£200 and can be used with a minimum of instruction.

The *urinary alcohol* concentration can also be measured: a value exceeding 120 mg/100 ml is suggestive and one over 200 mg/100 ml is diagnostic of alcoholism. The sample should be refrigerated and preferably frozen until analysis, otherwise false-positive results will be obtained, especially in diabetic patients, because of fermentation of glucose.

Conventional tests: no unequivocal values

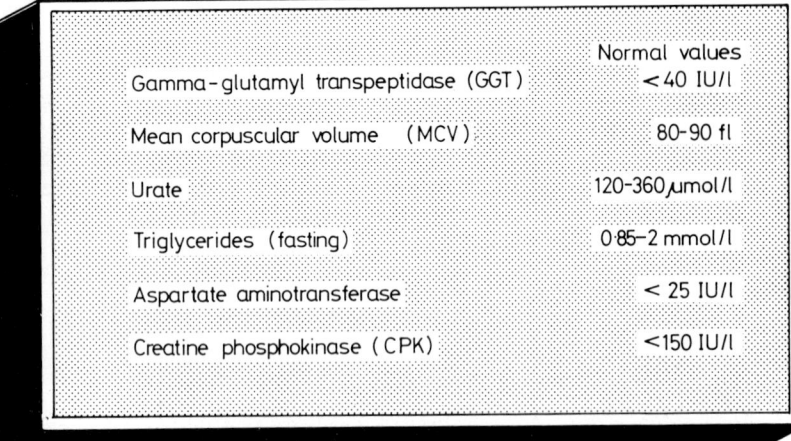

	Normal values
Gamma-glutamyl transpeptidase (GGT)	< 40 IU/l
Mean corpuscular volume (MCV)	80-90 fl
Urate	120-360 μmol/l
Triglycerides (fasting)	0·85-2 mmol/l
Aspartate aminotransferase	< 25 IU/l
Creatine phosphokinase (CPK)	<150 IU/l

None of the conventional laboratory tests, either alone or in combination, can give an unequivocal indication of alcohol abuse. Those which are highly sensitive are not invariably abnormal. They are affected by other diseases, in particular of the liver, blood, heart, and kidneys, and by drugs, especially those which induce enzymes, such as barbiturates, anticonvulsants, and steroid hormones. Nevertheless, if these causes can be excluded, abnormal values should alert the doctor to the possibility of alcohol abuse before there is physical damage and suggest to him that he should give advice about reducing alcohol intake or even abstaining altogether.

GGT and MCV

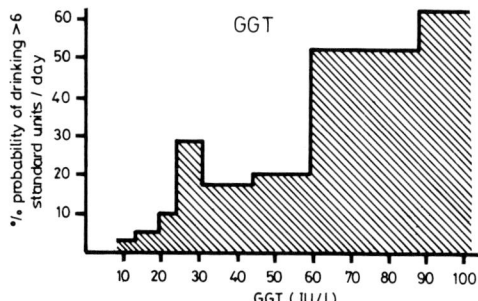

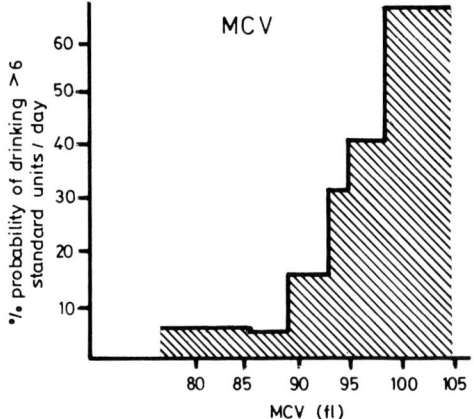

The most sensitive markers of alcoholism are the serum concentration of the enzyme gamma-glutamyl transpeptidase (GGT) and the red cell mean corpuscular volume (MCV). Together they will identify three out of four heavy drinkers. Supportive evidence may be obtained from measuring serum urate, fasting triglycerides, and the enzymes aspartate or alamine aminotransferase and creatinine phosphokinase.

Measurement of gamma-glutamyl transpeptidase activity is the best screening test available. Values above 40 IU/l are found in about 80% of problem drinkers, both men and women, whether or not there is demonstrable liver damage.

A mean corpuscular volume of more than 92 fl is found in about 60% of alcoholics and is more commonly raised in women than men. If other causes have been excluded, a raised mean corpuscular volume is especially meaningful, since the action of alcohol on the maturation of red cells differs from its effect on biochemical processes in the liver.

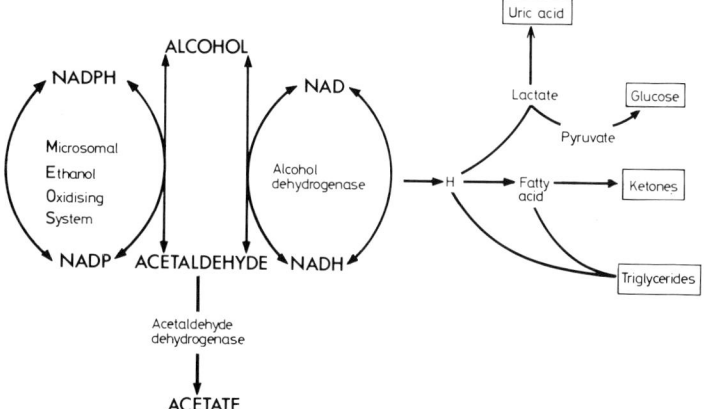

Other tests

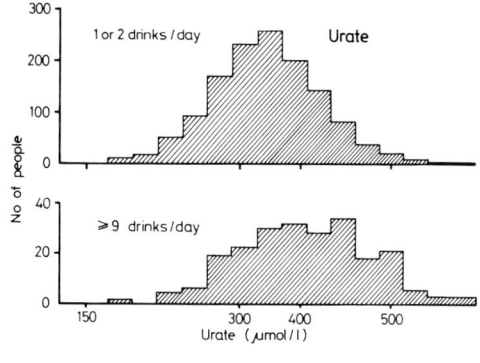

Urate concentrations (raised in about half of all heavy drinkers) and *triglycerides* may be usefully included in a screening profile in men, but they are poor discriminators of heavy drinking in women. A grossly lipaemic serum will sometimes indicate alcoholism.

Raised *aminotransferase* activities indicate liver damage rather than alcoholism, being present in over 95% of patients with alcoholic hepatitis and in half of those with fatty liver or cirrhosis.

Creatinine phosphokinase activity is raised in nearly half of all alcoholics; high values may result from bruising. Because it is not an index of liver function it provides a means of separating detection of alcoholism from detection of liver damage.

Biochemical and haematological profiles can be used to obtain an index of excessive alcohol intake. Increasing concentrations of each marker can be directly related to increasing alcohol intake, but they give only a statistical probability that a subject is abusing alcohol. Nevertheless, since their normal distribution is heavily skewed (most results being at the lower end) values in the upper range of normal should be viewed with suspicion if one marker—for example, mean corpuscular volume—is definitely abnormal.

Biochemical markers such as gamma-glutamyl transpeptidase activity return rapidly to normal with abstention from alcohol and may be misleading if measured 48 hours after the last drink. A subsequent rise of 50% or more is strong evidence of resumption of heavy drinking. The mean corpuscular volume, on the other hand, takes several weeks to return to normal after abstinence.

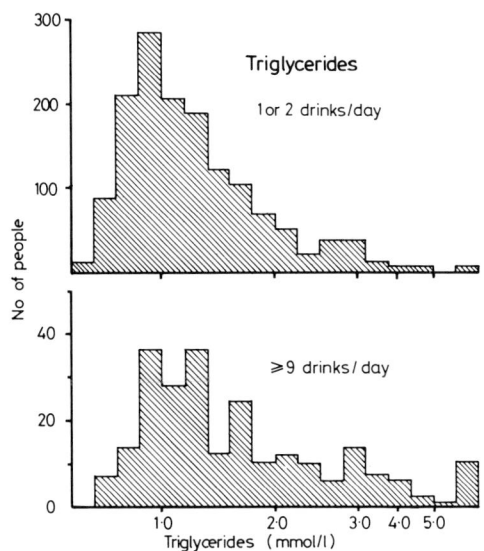

The photograph of the alcometers was reproduced by permission of Lion Laboratories Ltd, Barry, and the following diagrams by permission of their authors and editors: the diagram of ethanol metabolism was adapted from an article by Lieber CS. *N Engl J Med* 1978;**298**:356; those of GGT and MCV from an article by Chick J, Kreitman N, Plant M. *Lancet* 1981;i:1249-51; and those of urate and triglycerides from an article by Whitfield JB, Hensley WJ, Bryden D, Gallagher H. *Ann Clin Biochem* 1978;**15**:297-302.

DETECTION IN HOSPITAL

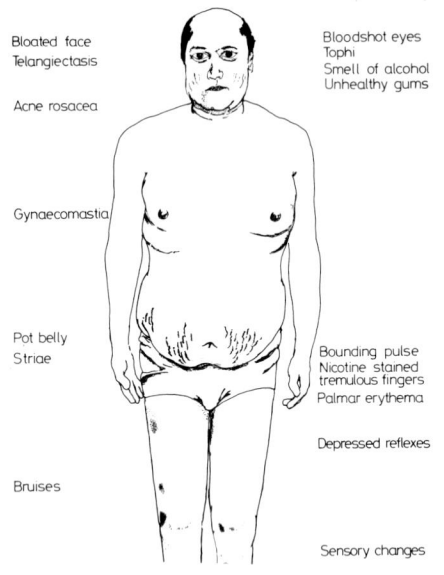

Bloated face
Telangiectasis

Acne rosacea

Gynaecomastia

Pot belly
Striae

Bruises

Bloodshot eyes
Tophi
Smell of alcohol
Unhealthy gums

Bounding pulse
Nicotine stained
tremulous fingers
Palmar erythema

Depressed reflexes

Sensory changes

Alcoholism has replaced syphilis as the great mimic of disease. Its protean symptoms are compounded by the reluctance of many patients, relatives, and doctors to accept that there is a problem. In addition the medical approach is that of the doctor looking for gross signs of disease of the liver, heart, brain, or other organs. To concentrate on these is deceptive and unhelpful. By the time they are present the disease may be irreversible, and their absence gives a false sense of security.

A few people are referred to hospital about their drinking habits; and a few, who may or may not be known to abuse alcohol, are referred because of hepatomegaly or abnormal liver function values. These are the minority. Most people who turn out to be problem drinkers have non-specific symptoms which are often vague, multiple, and do not fit readily into any diagnostic pattern; sometimes they may be bizarre. Gastrointestinal symptoms, chest and abdominal pain, and neuropsychiatric disturbances are the most common, but any system may be affected.

Spotting the problem drinker

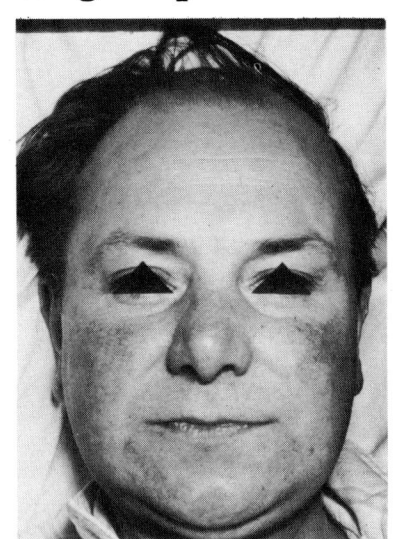

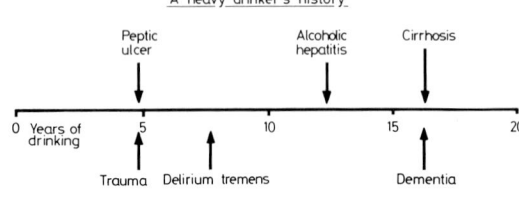

A heavy drinker's history

Peptic
ulcer

Alcoholic
hepatitis

Cirrhosis

0 Years of   5   10   15   20
   drinking

Trauma   Delirium tremens   Dementia

The problem drinker may be spotted by his brash, jocular, overfamiliar manner, inappropriate to the circumstances of a medical consultation. He may give shifty answers to preliminary questions, and it is important not to reveal any suspicions and lose his confidence. Symptoms should be regarded sympathetically and not brushed aside; they will often provide further clues.

Certain features in the history should also raise suspicions: absenteeism from work; frequent attendances for unexplained and atypical dyspepsia or for minor gastrointestinal bleeding; hospital admissions for accidents of all kinds or "head injury"; fits, "turns," falls, and neuritis (peripheral neuropathy).

Familial risk factors include alcoholism; teetotalism; depression, especially among women; a broken home; and being last in a large family. Drinking by the spouse, drug taking, and heavy cigarette smoking are often associated.

Ethnic origins should be considered. People of Irish and Scottish descent seem to drink more than the English and to be more prone to physical damage. Europeans may have a high prevalence of alcoholism because they are socially accustomed to high levels of drinking. Jews may drink but intoxication is frowned on. Moslems are, strictly speaking, forbidden by their religion to drink alcohol, but taboos are breaking down, especially among men. Oriental races are said to show exaggerated responses to alcohol.

Young men drink heavily, but in most it is a passing phase; girls may now be following suit. Many occupations are known to increase the risk of alcoholism; this may be due both to the nature of the job and to the individual who is attracted to it. Heavy drinkers are found in all occupations and in all classes of society.

Signs

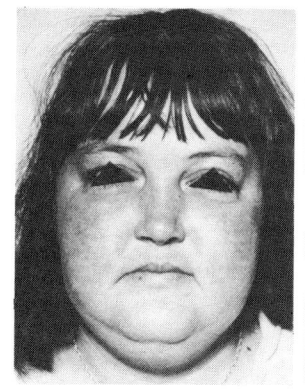
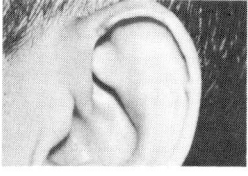
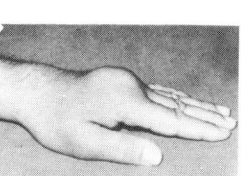
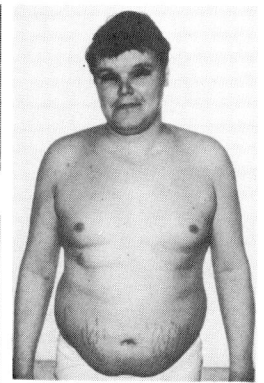
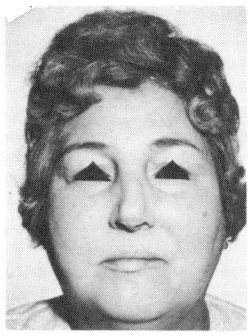
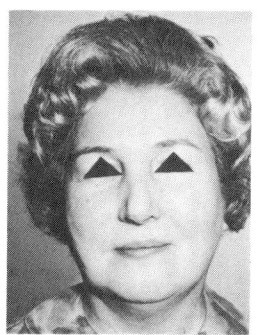

Before (left) and after (right) stopping drinking.

Certain signs may he helpful, if present: the bloated, plethoric face, with or without telangiectases or spider naevi; bloodshot conjunctivae; acne rosacea; smell of stale alcohol; and raw, red gums which may bleed readily. Facial appearances resembling those of Cushing's syndrome have been recognised recently.

The skin is warm and moist with a fast, bounding pulse, and marked tremor of nicotine-stained fingers (a pseudothyrotoxic state). Other signs, such as palmar erythema, bilateral Dupuytren's contractures, parotid swelling (rare), and gouty tophi, should be sought. Obesity, with a pot belly, gynaecomastia, and striae, are common. Bruising and scarring indicate recurrent falls and brawls.

The physical consequences of alcoholism are well known and this is not the place to discuss them. Successful medical intervention depends on diagnosis before irreversible damage has occurred, and the index of suspicion should be high that alcohol contributes to or causes the following:
Repeated attendance or admissions for relatively minor complaints which cannot be clearly labelled
Fits for the first time in middle age
Gout, whatever the immediate precipitating cause
Mild diabetic symptoms or glycosuria in the young or middle aged
About 15% of all "essential" hypertension, and failure to control the blood pressure with multiple drugs
Atypical cardiac symptoms or cardiac failure in middle-aged men
Attacks of confusion, especially in strange surroundings or after stress (illness, operation, bereavement, etc)
Drug overdoses
Gastrointestinal symptoms where a cause cannot be established
Hepatomegaly, for which no other cause can be found
Anaemia, especially if folate deficient
Lobar pneumonia, especially when it affects the right upper lobe
Atypical endocrine features mimicking Cushing's disease, phaeochromocytoma, and carcinoid.

	Complaints	Mistaken for	Due to
Gastrointestinal			
	Indigestion		Oesophagitis
	Heartburn		Gastritis
	Vomiting	Peptic ulcer	Enteritis
	Diarrhoea	Viral hepatitis	Mallory Weiss
	Bleeding	Gall stones	syndrome
	Jaundice		Pancreatitis
			Alcoholic hepatitis/ cirrhosis
Neuropsychiatric			
	Trembling		Withdrawal symptoms
	Sweating		Hypoglycaemia
	Insomnia		Depression
	Headaches		Acute psychosis
	Blackouts	Neurasthenia	Encephalopathy
	Fits	Anxiety state	Neuromyopathy
	Confusion	Epilepsy	Dementia
	Inability to concentrate		Alcohol poisoning
	Burning legs		Drug abuse
	Coma		Subdural haematoma
Cardiorespiratory			
	Palpitations	Ischaemic heart disease	Arrhythmias
	Chest pain		Cardiomyopathy
	Bronchitis	Essential hypertension	Upper lobe pneumonia
	Pneumonia		Tuberculosis
Musculoskeletal			
	Backache		
	Rheumatism	Idiopathic gout	Gout
	Gout	Accidents	Demineralisation
	Repeated injuries		
Skin			
	Acne rosacea		
	Athlete's foot		
	Sweat rash		
Hormonal and metabolic			
	Obesity	Cushing's syndrome	
	"Sugar"	Diabetes mellitus	
	Breast swelling	Breast tumour	
	Reduced libido	Phaechromocytoma	
	Infertility	Carcinoid	
Pregnancy			
	Repeated stillbirths		Fetal alcohol syndrome
	Congenital lesions		

DETECTION IN GENERAL PRACTICE

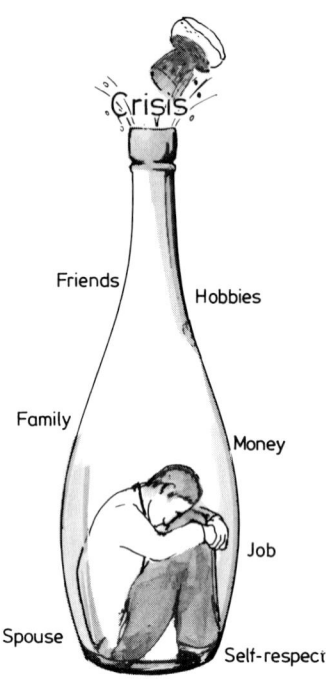

The problems of detecting alcoholism include the conceptual difficulty of defining it and the practical difficulty of identifying the excessive drinker. A working definition for general practice might be: the devotion of time to alcohol instead of to oneself or one's family, friends, hobbies, and job. The drinker hides the extent of his drinking from himself; those around him may suspect or know that he drinks but cannot discuss it with him and may collude in concealing it.

Diagnosis is a process of pattern recognition. We have a mental image of the "alcoholic" as a man aged 30-60 who, after years of heavy drinking, has isolated himself from the normal sources of social and personal support by a series of crises, in one of which the general practitioner becomes involved. This damaged person feels different from us and the hurt he causes alienates our sympathy. We see the problems but have previously missed their beginnings. There are several other pictures.

Portraits of problem drinkers

Teenagers with drinking problems are seldom seen in the surgery but may be known to the police for drinking under age or drink-driving offences. Parents may complain that they are out a lot, lethargic, and difficult at home.

Housewives take to drink because they feel lonely or unvalued and this leads to sexual discord, family friction, and even drinking husbands. Women who work outside the home are also at risk, especially in competitive jobs.

The elderly are prone to physical deterioration, intellectual failure, and social isolation. The drinking may be lost in the confusion.

The respected use their status to conceal and their intelligence to rationalise trouble. Regard for them diminishes the critical powers of colleagues, and false loyalties may delay help.

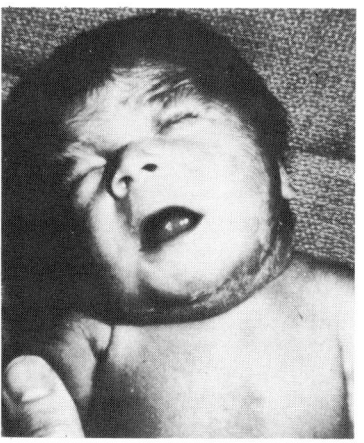 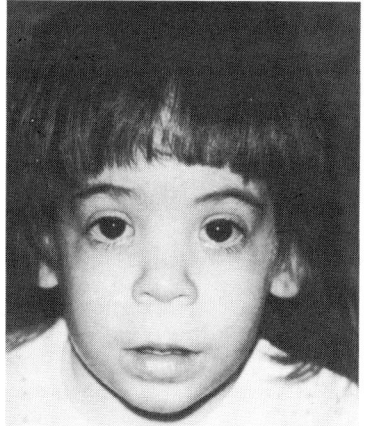

Children are the most vulnerable members of the family. Infants born to mothers who drink may be damaged. Excessive drinking by the mother in pregnancy is teratogenic and may also cause the fetal alcohol syndrome. Disordered communications cause developmental delay (due to lack of input) or non-accidental injury (violent input). If parents do not respond to simple advice about a child's problems, the general practitioner should ask himself where the block is: alcohol could be the hidden cause.

Members of the family are often the presenting sign of a drinking problem, but their prodromal approach is frequently missed. The general practitioner treats the symptoms without recognising the underlying cause. Non-drinking members of the family suffer too, are patients, and need our care. They are often the best way into a drinking problem, and yield the first rewards for efforts to help.

Identification

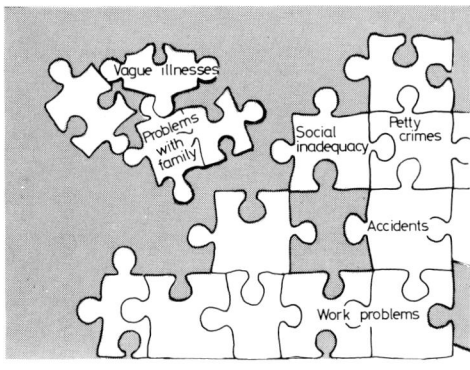

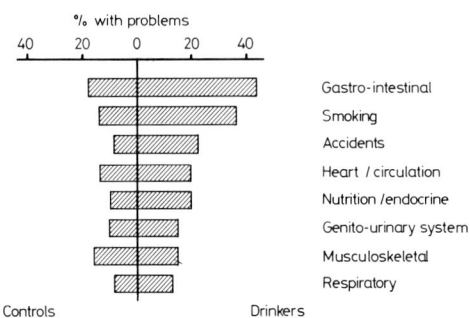

% with problems	
40 20 0 20 40	Gastro-intestinal
	Smoking
	Accidents
	Heart / circulation
	Nutrition /endocrine
	Genito-urinary system
	Musculoskeletal
	Respiratory
Controls Drinkers	

How ?
When ?
Has it ever caused problems ?

All general practitioners share the salutary experience of having treated a patient for years without recognising their dependence on alcohol. We need to raise our index of suspicion by asking ourselves early and every time whether alcohol abuse could be contributing to the patients' illness. The pattern for problem drinking is a constellation of clues, no one diagnostic in itself but together indicating that alcohol in the patient or someone close to him is the probable underlying factor.

The physical complaints of heavy drinkers are frequently vague and without demonstrable organic cause: loss of appetite, tummy upsets, morning shakes, sweats, backache, memory lapses, and accidents. Signs of psychological incompetence include unhappiness, erratic moods, sexual failure, family conflicts, confusion, and "going on the wagon." Social inadequacy is shown by requests for a sickness certificate, underachievement, out-of-character behaviour, work problems, money shortage, and trouble with the law.

The patient must be asked how much he drinks, when, how often, and whether his drinking has ever caused problems. If he resents such questions, why does he do so? The drink lessens his feelings of isolation and worthlessness, and because he sees his problems as the cause and not the result of his drinking he may become aggressive or clamp down if this solution is threatened. These are physical signs and should not irritate the doctor.

The doctor should ask himself whether an attitude of disapproval will help. He should be direct and specific, challenging any vagueness, wariness, evasion, inconsistencies, bluff, or facile assurances.

The patient will not give a true answer until he can be honest with himself. If he will talk the doctor should encourage any sign that he is beginning to examine himself. Progress depends on his confidence in the doctor, and on the doctor's sensitivity as to when the patient is ready to accept some insight.

The doctor should watch out for the gaps of what is not said and for non-verbal signs—a swallow, a flush, or sudden stillness. Physical signs include a smell of alcohol or peppermint, obesity, sweating, shakes, rapid pulse, liver palms, a tender liver, and injuries, either to the drinker himself or to others, the cause of which he will usually deny.

Detection in general practice

Records

Date	★	CLINICAL NOTES
6.7.79		Indigestion. Appetite good. Smoking 30/day Advised mag. trisil
2.1.81		Bruised hand. Tender ® 5th MP joint. No deformity. Reassured
2.3.81		Irritable — overworking (self-employed now) — not sleeping
		Nitrazepam ㉚
12.8.81		Came late to discuss son's school refusal — slammed out when asked to wait
3.9.81		More stomach pains — depressed — in laws critical Smoking ↑ 40 Drinks × 2 weekly — social
15.9.81		Hands shaky. check blood for MCV + δGT Last week wife walked out with children Patient turned car over. Breathalyser + Blood alcohol awaited. Stands to lose his business (taxi). States alcohol no problem — has been dry since! Resists referral — just wants children back

★ This column has been provided for doctors to enter A, V or C at their discretion.

THIS RECORD IS THE PROPERTY OF THE SECRETARY OF STATE FOR SOCIAL SERVICES

Records are the general practitioner's paper instruments for detecting problem drinkers. Their value depends on the quality of the recording, the ease of retrieval by arrangement in chronological order, and the existence of summaries and cross references to the records of other members of the family. Patterns of presentation suggesting problem drinking may fit our template. Evidence of stress, frequent consultations, loss of communication within the family, and changes of spouse, address, or doctor provide further clues. Specific test results, such as a high mean corpuscular volume (MCV) on a previous routine blood count or an abnormal liver function value may complete the pattern.

Bilirubin	S.G.O.T.			
10	25	4 ·63	RBC x 10¹²/l	
µmol/l	units			
5 – 17	< 25	16 · 2	Hb g/dl	
Glucose	δ–GT	· 48 . 6	PCV	
	55.6	105 ·	MCV fl	
mmol/l	units	34 · 9	MCH pg	
2·5 – 4·7 fasting	M6–28 F4–18	33 · 3	MCHC g/dl	

8 · 8	WBC x 10⁹/l

Eth

Tre

M.C

FILM — Additi

Communications

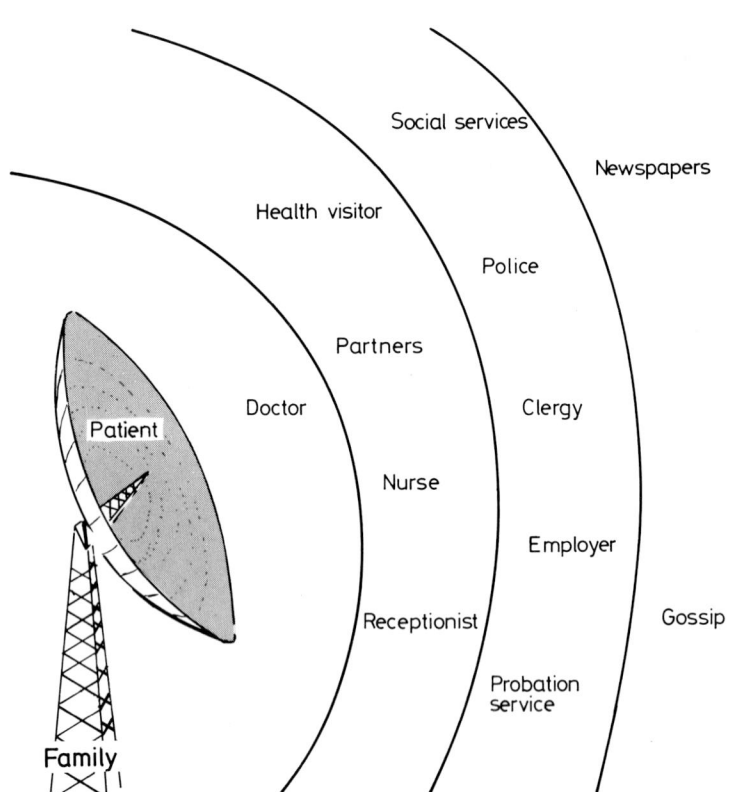

Social services
Newspapers
Health visitor
Police
Partners
Doctor
Clergy
Patient
Nurse
Employer
Receptionist
Gossip
Family
Probation service

Other sources of information are part of the general practitioner's network of communications. He is in a unique position to recognise alcoholism in its early and remediable stages, and listening does not compromise confidentiality. He must avoid both the wasteful pursuit of an illness-centred diagnosis, and the neglect of any opportunity to assume his responsibility for the *health* of those families who have entrusted themselves to his care.

> Members of the primary care team have considerable opportunity to identify problem drinkers. The aim must be that not only shall they do this but they shall also provide treatment and care.
>
> Advisory Committee on Alcoholism 1978

The illustrations of fetal alcohol syndrome were reproduced by permission from an article by Sterling K Clarren *JAMA* 1981;**245**:2436-9 and that of percentage of drinkers with various medical problems from an article by I C Buchan and others *J R Coll Gen Pract* 1981;**31**:151-3.

HELPING THE PROBLEM DRINKER

Other articles in this series have shown that alcohol is a health issue and that patients' drinking habits are, like smoking, a matter for clinical inquiry. The doctor has a responsibility to advise his patients about sensible drinking and to recognise alcohol-related problems at an early stage.

Many people are sensitive about their drinking, and the offer of help will be more readily accepted if it is given in a spirit of concern for health and the family's wellbeing. It is usually misplaced to be judgemental, and dire warnings are rarely heeded unless they occur in a setting of mutual trust and respect. Once these preconditions exist simple advice from the general practitioner about changing habits is often surprisingly effective.

How to help and how to motivate

BALANCE SHEET		
Drinking	Advantages	Disadvantages
Continue	Forget my worries Escape responsibility	Lose family Health deteriorates Cost
Reduce	Be like others Appear "normal"	I found it hard and failed last time. Wife expects me to abstain and doesn't believe it possible
Stop	Please wife Health improves Save money	What to do with my time. What to tell my drinking friends

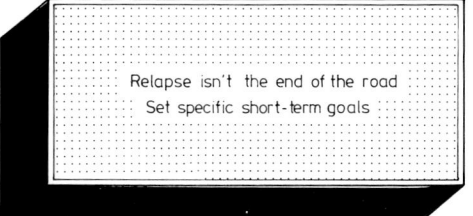

Relapse isn't the end of the road
Set specific short-term goals

Most doctors are pessimistic about being able to help alcoholics, yet there is good evidence that as many as two-thirds respond well to treatment. The family doctor is ideally placed to recognise the problem early and intervene.

Motivation is a rather suspect concept. We often blame the patient for lack of motivation when relapse occurs, but, in common with many medical conditions, the treatment of alcohol problems is characterised by relapses and remissions. Relapse is not necessarily the end of the therapeutic road, and the strength of motivation is certainly not constant. A reluctant patient brought by a desperate spouse or coming to avoid dismissal from work can often be converted into taking a personal responsibility for stopping or reducing his or her drinking.

The patient has acquired a drinking habit which is damaging his personality, his family and social life, or his health. Our habits are often hard to change, and the patient will be ambivalent about changing his drinking pattern. This ambivalence can often be addressed directly by asking the patient to draw up a balance sheet of the good and bad consequences of his continued drinking.

Armed with such evidence the patient should set realistic goals for changing his or her lifestyle. It is best to aim for specific short-term goals at first so that the patient gets a sense of achievement by attaining, for instance, three weeks' abstinence or even a party negotiated without disgrace and then reporting progress. This is often preferable to global but ill-considered promises such as, "I shall never touch another drop." Alcoholics Anonymous embodies the good sense of this approach in its recommendation that the alcoholic should take "only one day at a time."

Helping the problem drinker

Changing the lifestyle: impediments

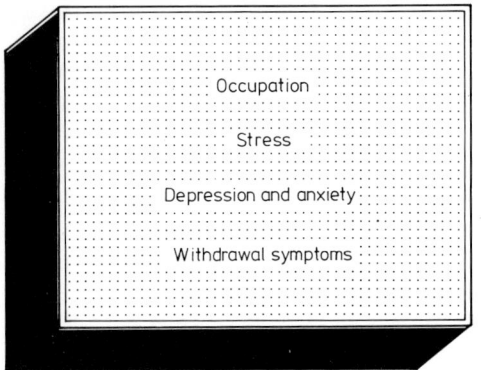

For many problem drinkers drinking has become their predominant interest; to achieve the desired goal they will in time have to make major changes in their way of life. The patient will need help to look at impediments to change and alternatives to drinking.

The impediments will either be evident from the initial balance sheet or become clearer as the drinker tries to change his habits. Impediments may be, for example, a job where drink is readily available, family stress which the drinker cannot cope with without alcohol, an established neurosis or depression which has been masked by drinking, or the occurrence of withdrawal symptoms when he tries to stop drinking. The patient should look out for situations and feelings which "trigger off" drinking and work out new ways of coping with them.

Changing the lifestyle: alternatives to drinking

At its simplest patients can be asked to think of activities they enjoy which do not involve drinking. The answer to this question may initially be "none." Alternatives often become clearer if specific attention is paid to past triggers for drinking—for example, the drink at the end of the day may be avoided by going home earlier, the pre-match drink by meeting at the ground itself, and so on. Anxiety as a trigger to drinking may be relieved by appropriate relaxation training. Sometimes more elaborate help focused, for example, on tensions in the family may be necessary. The clinician should not discount the more obvious seemingly mechanical and naive solutions, which often prove surprisingly effective.

Involve the spouse

The spouse is often the prime mover in getting help for the patient. He or she should be actively involved in consultations, partly as an additional source of evidence about the true state of affairs and as an aid to helping the family find a new way of life that does not involve drinking.

The family will have made certain protective adaptations to cope with its drinking members and will need to adjust to the new abstinent personality in its midst. Trust takes time to be re-established and the family will often need support during periods of relapse in which the spouse may feel that all is irretrievably lost. The spouse of an alcoholic often feels confused, bitter, and devalued and will welcome the chance of being understood and participating in the process of recovery.

To drink or not to drink

The goal of intervention will depend on the extent of the patient's drinking problem. If the drinking is excessive but hitherto harm-free, the doctor should advise about safe limits for drinking, such as "two or three pints a day two or three times a week," keeping in mind the evidence that those who regularly drink more than five pints of beer or its equivalent daily are seriously endangering their health.

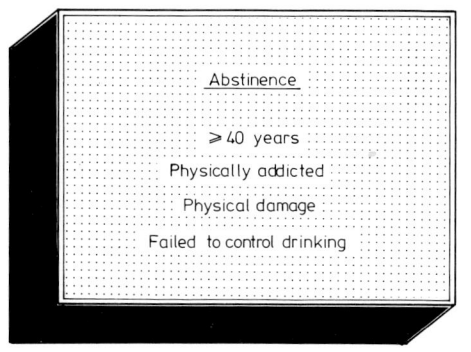

Abstence

≥ 40 years

Physically addicted

Physical damage

Failed to control drinking

Some drinkers with established problems will return to moderate harm-free drinking, but it is difficult to predict who will succeed where others fail. Present evidence suggests that abstinence remains the preferred goal for those who are over 40, are seriously physically addicted, have evidence of physical damage, or have tried controlled drinking treatment without success. For younger people whose problem drinking has been detected at an early stage and who are not seriously addicted or damaged modified drinking may be a more acceptable and feasible goal.

Most specialists have probably become less insistent on abstinence as the goal and are willing to consider modified drinking. This needs to be carefully planned and discussed and is best preceded by a period of abstinence until evidence of physical harm has disappeared.

Review

Week commencing ___25 May___ 1981

Record exactly what you have drunk on each day last week

	Beers (pints)	Spirits (glasses)	Others including wine (glasses)	Place where consumed
Monday	3			Pub at lunchtime
Tuesday	4	2 whiskies		Pub / friends/ evening
Wednesday				
Thursday	8			Evening / friends / pay day
Friday	4 (lunchtime) 5 (evening)	2 whiskies		Row with wife
Saturday	2 (lunchtime)		1 bottle wine (dinner)	Home with wife
Sunday	2 (lunchtime)	2 whiskies (evening)		Pub with wife and friends

Whatever the agreed goals, it is essential that the doctor regularly reviews the patient's progress. The most important task at the first interview is to gain the patient's interest in tackling his or her drinking problem and to ensure that he or she returns for the next appointment. At this time the short-term achievements and problems can be reviewed and further goals agreed.

Supportive laboratory tests (γ-glutamyl transpeptidase, mean corpuscular volume, and blood alcohol) are useful objective means of monitoring progress, and the results and their implications should be discussed with the patient. A diary in which the patient makes a note of any drinks consumed, the time, their quantity, and the occasion is a useful aid to self-audit.

Progress should be reviewed regularly over a year. The first six months of progress often give a good impression of longer term prognosis.

Relapse

What happened – a behavioural analysis

When ?

Where ?

Who was there ?

How much did I drink ?

How often did I drink ?

Most patients will drink again whatever the original goal of treatment but this need not be a catastrophic relapse involving the loss of all that has been achieved. It is more profitably viewed as an opportunity for the patient to learn more about the nature of himself and the problem. Dealing with and learning from relapses is part of recovery. It needs to be taken seriously by the doctor and patient, and the questions shown opposite need to be honestly asked and answered. Once the anatomy of a relapse is laid bare in this way the patient can recognise strategies for preventing a recurrence.

A closer study of relapses should help patient and doctor to identify triggers to drinking, which may be listed. The family often feels particularly threatened and confused by a relapse and will need extra support at this time.

HELP: DRUGS

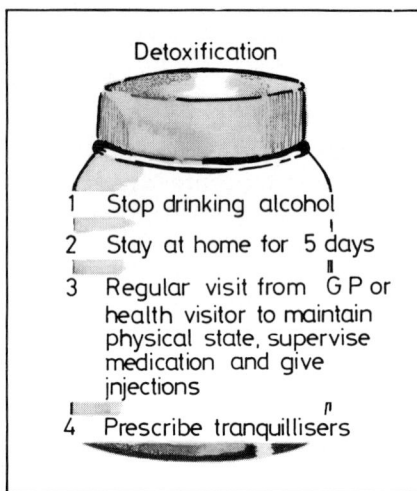

Detoxification

1 Stop drinking alcohol
2 Stay at home for 5 days
3 Regular visit from G P or health visitor to maintain physical state, supervise medication and give injections
4 Prescribe tranquillisers

20 mg qds chlordiazepoxide
or 2 mg qds lorazepam
or 5 mg qds diazepam
or 3 capsules qds chlormethiazole

Stop

Monday Tuesday Wednesday Thursday Friday Saturday Sunday

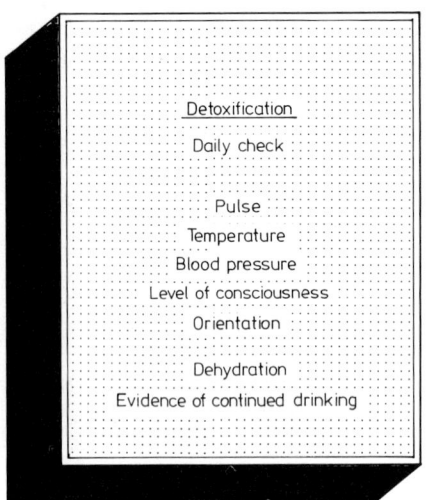

Detoxification

Daily check

Pulse
Temperature
Blood pressure
Level of consciousness
Orientation

Dehydration
Evidence of continued drinking

The previous article emphasised the importance of gaining the patient's trust and ensuring that regular contact is retained while he endeavours to change his lifestyle. Drugs have very little place in the long-term management of alcohol problems. They have three principal indications.

Detoxification

Detoxification for the patient who is physically dependent on alcohol may be achieved at home if the patient is willing to stay off work for five days and has a reasonably supportive family. A suitable regimen is shown. Benzodiazepines may be given in a dose that reduces over one week and then stops. Chlormethiazole in a similar regimen may be used, but dependence is a danger if treatment is prolonged, and severe reactions with alcohol may occur. The dose prescribed and the rate of reduction should be related to the clinical state of the patient, but it is not necessary to continue tranquillisers beyond one week. Tranquillisers must not be given on a long-term basis, and the patient should not take them when he is drinking.

Vitamins—Multivitamin preparations are helpful and are best given intramuscularly because impaired absorption is common: dose 7 ml Parentrovite daily for 6 days. Thereafter oral vitamins should be given for one month. If there is evidence of organic brain damage or vitamin depletion this course should be prolonged.

Anticonvulsants—Phenytoin 50 mg three times a day may be given prophylactically over one week to patients with a history of withdrawal seizures.

Alcohol sensitisation

Disulfiram (Antabuse) 200 mg daily or citrated calcium carbimide (Abstem) 100 mg daily is used to sensitise the body to alcohol. The patient who takes one of these drugs and drinks experiences flushing, headache, palpitations, nausea, faintness, and collapse. The reaction may be severe and patients who have established heart disease should not take these drugs; neither should those who are very impulsive or suicidal. All patients should carry a warning card explaining the dangers of taking alcohol with these drugs. Patients who can establish the habit of taking Antabuse or Abstem find it a useful aid to abstinence.

Psychiatric disorders

Alcohol abuse is sometimes a symptom of an underlying and treatable psychiatric disorder. Depressive illness is a common precipitant in women and responds to appropriate antidepressants. Alcohol dependence is itself a depressing condition, however, and symptoms of depression usually recede when the drinking stops.

HELP: REFERRAL

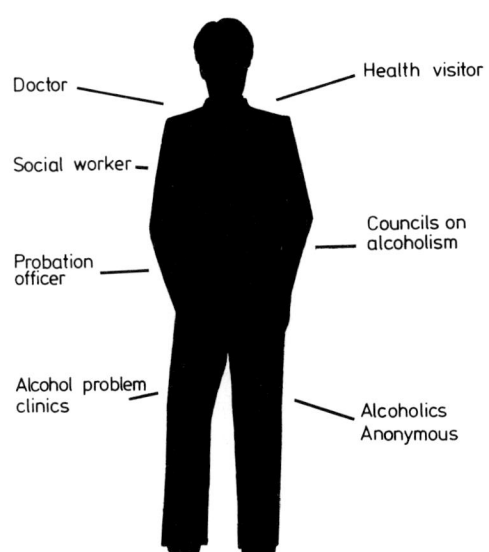

Doctor

Health visitor

Social worker

Councils on alcoholism

Probation officer

Alcohol problem clinics

Alcoholics Anonymous

General practitioners may feel that they do not have time to counsel the problem drinker within a busy practice but this view may not be fully justified. Firstly, the GP already knows a lot about the patient and his family and can focus questions and advice quickly. Secondly, the interviews, apart from the assessment with the spouse, which may take 30 minutes, can be conducted in an ordinary surgery. It is probably better to have most interviews short but frequent. Thirdly, the GP has a position of trust and authority, both crucial factors in securing compliance. Finally, the patient and his family will attend the surgery anyway—complaining of the symptoms of excessive drinking—so the GP might just as well tackle the underlying cause as patch up the consequences.

When and where to refer

(1) Severe withdrawal symptoms, particularly fits or delirium tremens—this is an emergency.

(2) Lack of supportive environment for withdrawal.

(3) Suspected damage such as decompensated liver disease, peripheral neuropathy, brain damage.

(4) Patient not responding to the approach outlined in this and the previous article.

(5) Presence of underlying neurosis or psychosis.

(6) Very disturbed or unsupportive family.

(7) Need for help in restructuring social activities.

(8) Request for more help with counselling.

As well as the general practitioner, other members of his team, such as health visitors, district nurses, and social workers, are also in a position to take action. The primary care team is thus ideally placed for early intervention, and this alone is often enough. But referral may be necessary, and a variety of agencies and specialist services (see below) provide a network of support for alcoholics, though they can never cater for all the problem drinkers in Great Britain.

When referral does take place it is important to maintain a relationship with the patient, or he may feel that he is a parcel being passed from one agency to another. It is important to explain the reasons for referral and to check the patient's expectations. Finally, give the patient a further appointment after his consultation with the hospital or other agency so that you can check whether he in fact attended (many do not) and discuss his views about this new contact.

Alcohol problem clinics (alcoholism treatment units)

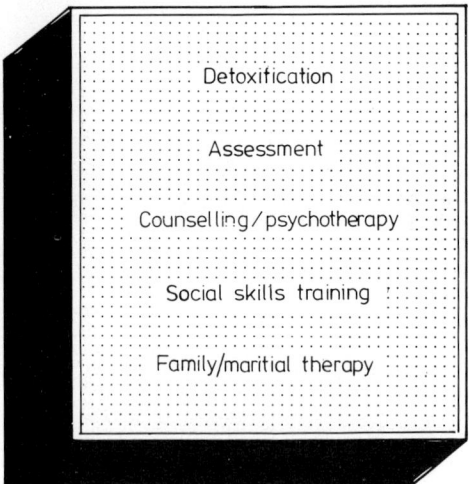

These are usually associated with psychiatric units; they or district general hospitals have facilities for detoxification. They provide not only specialist consultant services but also training for all types of staff, including volunteers. The services they offer vary considerably, but they generally offer a range of approaches to treatment. As there is no evidence that prolonged inpatient treatment is particularly effective there is an increasing emphasis on outpatient treatment. Many clinics offer drop-in facilities for patients and relatives and act as day centres. In general the approach has shifted away from being exclusively centered on group psychotherapy and Alcoholics Anonymous to incorporate counselling, marital therapy, training in social skills, and educational approaches.

The simplest advice is to get to know your local unit; the staff will also know about other services in the area.

Alcoholics Anonymous, Al-Anon, and Al-Alteen

Alcoholics Anonymous, 3 Birchfield Rd 19..............021-523 9310
ALCOHOLICS ANONYMOUS 24 HOUR SERVICE,
Walmley.........021 378 0607
Alcoholics Anonymous & Al-Anon 29......................021 475 1817
Alcoholism Information Centre, 32 Essex St 5.........021 622 2041

Alcoholics Anonymous exists throughout Britain; and its membership is growing at the rate of 15% a year. It asks members to acknowledge that they are alcoholic and that abstinence is the only way towards recovery. Some are deterred by its quasi-religious undertones, but there is no requirement to worship or accept religion. Many patients dismiss AA before they have attended often enough to benefit from the fellowship it offers. It is often necessary to shop around before finding a group that suits a particular personality. The GP should get to know a few AA members personally and refer his patients to them. This is much more effective than an open suggestion to attend AA, which many patients are reluctant to do. Some branches man a telephone 24 hours; the number can be found in the local directory.

Al-Anon and Al-Alteen are less familiar organisations, which provide support for, respectively, the spouses and teenage children of alcoholics. They can attend in their own right without the patient necessarily belonging to AA. They are especially valuable where heavy drinking has disrupted the family and caused loss of self-esteem and problems over money, care of children, and disposal of property.

Councils on alcoholism

National Council on Alcoholism
    3 Grosvenor Crescent, London SW1X 7EE
    Telephone 01-235-4182

Scottish Council on Alcoholism,
    147 Blythswood Street, Glasgow G2 4EN
    Telephone 041 333 9677

Northern Ireland Council on Alcoholism,
    36-40 Victoria Square, Belfast 1
    Telephone 0232 38173/38202

Many areas have established local councils on alcoholism, which are voluntary agencies whose responsibilities include co-ordinating available services and educating and training of voluntary counsellors. They also provide free counselling and advice to problem drinkers and their families and many organise social activities for recovering problem drinkers. Councils will provide information about where to obtain help: some areas have an alcohol information service listed in the telephone directory.

Hostels

Hostels are provided by some local authorities and by voluntary bodies. They cater principally but not exclusively for homeless alcoholics and also provide a halfway house for alcoholics discharged from hospital. They have facilities for counselling and rehabilitation. Most require abstinence as a condition of residence. In large cities night shelter accommodation is provided for the vagrant alcoholics, who have particular difficulties because they not only need to break away from alcohol but also lack any social framework within which to change. Information about hostels and detoxification centres for drunkenness offenders may be obtained from the Federation of Alcoholic Rehabilitation Establishments (FARE) or social work departments.

Probation service

Drunken offenders and people charged with drink-related crimes occupy a great deal of the time of police, courts, and prisons. Drunks arrested and detained in police custody are normally brought before the magistrates the next day; few are referred to the probation service unless they are already under supervision. About a quarter of the clients of the probation service have alcohol problems, and the majority of these people are aged 21-30.

The probation service has contributed to some initiatives in prevention and treatment. It has, for example, a detoxification centre in Leeds, and in Birmingham an experimental wet alcoholic reception centre has recently been opened. Changes in the Criminal Justice Act have given police the powers to take drunks to a place where they can dry out rather than arrest them, but so far the Birmingham wet centre is the only such "designated place" that exists. It has 12 beds and nursing staff experienced in the management of alcohol. Although it is mainly designed for use by the police, the centre will also accept individuals referred from other sources. Counselling and practical help are provided.

Alcohol at work

Bodies concerned with alcoholism

Alcohol Education Centre, 99 Denmark Hill, London SE5 8AZ
Medical Council on Alcoholism, 3 Grosvenor Crescent, London SW1X 7EE
(education and medical research)
Federation of Alcohol Rehabilitation Establishments, 3 Grosvenor Crescent, London SW1X 7EE

Sources

Davies DL. *Countdown on drinking*. London: BMA, 1980.
DHSS. *Prevention and health: drinking sensibly*. London: HMSO. 1981.
Edwards G, Grant M, eds. *Alcoholism treatment in transition*. London: Croom Helm, 1980.
Kendell RE. Alcoholism: a medical or a political problem. *Br Med J* 1979;i: 367-71.
Kessel N, Walton H. *Alcoholism*. Harmondsworth: Penguin, 1979.
Royal College of Psychiatrists. *Alcohol and Alcoholism*. London: Tavistock, 1979.
Taylor D. *Alcohol. Reducing the harm*. London: Office of Health Economics, 1981.
Wilson P. *Drinking in England and Wales. A survey by the Office of Population and Census Surveys*. London: HMSO, 1980.

The perspective of these articles has been mainly focused on the family doctor, but hospital doctors and casualty staff are often well placed to offer some of the help and advice described. In the future occupational health services will probably take on more responsibility for recognising and responding to alcohol problems at work. An increasing number of firms are adopting joint union-management policies to help problem drinkers at work. They guarantee job security to those willing to opt for treatment for their alcohol problem, and early reports suggest that this form of "constructive coercion" is effective.

ALCOHOL AND ALCOHOLISM

RICHARD SMITH MB

Assistant editor, *British Medical Journal*

OVERTURE TO THE ALCOHOL DEBATE

When *World Medicine* asked six well-known doctors how they should spend their last minutes if the nuclear bombs were dropping four of them in the few sentences allotted mentioned drinking alcohol.[1] Though the feature was hardly serious, it is one illustration of how important alcohol is today. In the last 20 years alcohol consumption in Britain has roughly doubled (figure) and the same trend has been seen in most Western countries.[2] From 1960 to 1972 world production of beer increased by 68%, of spirits by 61%, and of wine by 19%.[3] The drink industry two years ago was predicting that this trend would continue: whisky consumption was expected to rise between 1978 and 1991 by 6-32% and beer consumption by 21% between 1977 and 1988.* Associated with the increase in consumption has been an increase in the many forms of individual and social damage associated with alcohol.[2] Also rising is the concern of those most closely associated with alcohol problems, and a bandwagon to reduce the harm is rolling.

Alcohol problems have moved on to the agendas of many international, professional, and governmental committees. In the last four years the World Health Organisation Expert Committee,[4] the Department of Health and Social Security Advisory Committee on Alcoholism,[5] the House of Commons Expenditure Committee,[6] the Royal College of Psychiatrists,[2] and, most recently, the Central Policy Review Staff (the Government "think tank")[7] have considered the problem. All have reached similar conclusions and have recommended that the Government at the very least should not allow alcohol consumption to rise any further. No radical action has yet been taken, however: indeed the think tank report was suppressed. But if alcohol consumption and harm continue to rise then the Government may eventually be obliged to act.

These committees have begun to consider alcohol problems not only because alcohol-related harm is increasing but also because our understanding of alcohol problems has undergone a revolution in the last 20 years. In the years after the second world war consumption and damage were both comparatively low, and in the heady days of the first antibiotics and the appearance of the National Health Service few health workers or scientists in Britain were much interested in alcohol problems. Alcoholism was assumed to be a disease that affected only a small proportion of the population, who were peculiar in some genetic, biochemical, or psychological way. This idea was acceptable to both alcoholics, who were better off being thought

*In fact, in the second quarter of 1981 beer production in Britain was down by 7·8% compared with the same quarter for 1980. Wine consumption increased by about 11% in 1980, however, and spirit consumption rose by about 5%. The Brewers' Society thinks that beer production has fallen because of the recession, continuing inflation, tax increases, and the poor weather early this summer. It does not think that the fall will continue, but prediction is a difficult art in such uncertain times.

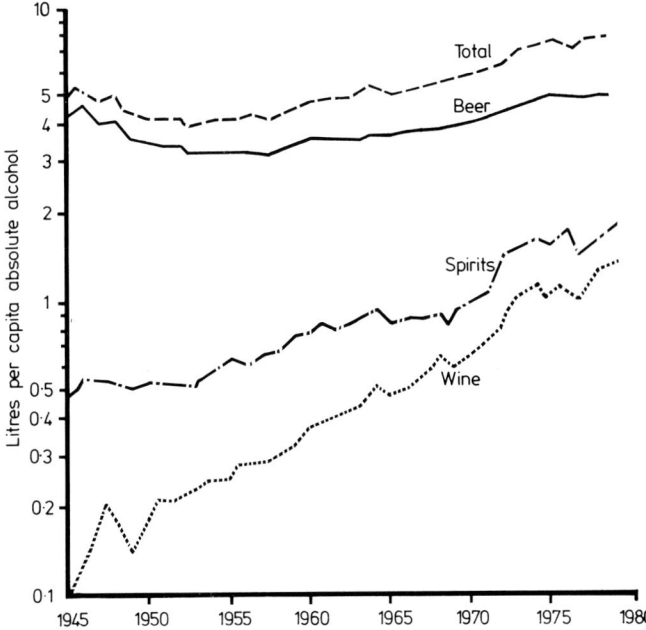

Beer, spirit, wine, and total alcohol consumption in Britain from 1945-79 (source: Office of Health Economics[18]).

sick rather than bad, and the drink trade, who could push alcohol sales confident that most people could not be harmed. No evidence was available to support this concept of alcoholism—it was simply assumed to be so.

Alcohol is what matters

Now that data have become available from around the world on how individuals and societies use alcohol these old ideas have changed. Separating alcoholics from non-alcoholics has proved to be impossible. The drinking pattern of many groups has been surveyed, and graphs showing how much people drink are always unimodal: there is no discrete population of individuals who drink more than everybody else.[8] Furthermore, longitudinal studies have shown that individuals can begin to drink more and move into a phase where they have symptoms associated with alcohol dependence, and, conversely, if they begin to drink less they can move out of this phase.[9] Certainly some people and some groups—for example, women—are more vulnerable than others to damage by alcohol but it seems as if everybody, given sufficient alcohol, is capable of becoming dependent.

Another reason for health workers, researchers, and govern-

Overture to the alcohol debate

ments to concentrate on alcohol rather than alcoholism is the great range of alcohol-associated damage. As well as the physical and mental damage associated with long-term alcohol abuse there is all the damage associated with intoxication. Many of the people killed in accidents on the road, in the home, and at work are not alcohol addicts—they may be only occasional drinkers. Alcohol is also associated with suicide, crime, violence, family breakdown, self-poisoning, and various cancers: alcohol misuse is a social disease with medical complications. Few of these problems result directly from alcohol, however, and a society that consumed less alcohol would not necessarily have less suicide, crime, or violence.

But it does seem that most of the various measures of alcohol damage do correlate with a society's consumption of alcohol. Indeed, the French demographer Ledermann was so impressed by survey data showing the relationships between amount of alcohol consumed, the number of heavy drinkers, and the degree of alcohol-associated damage in various populations that he developed a mathematical model to explain the relations.[10] His mathematics have since been criticised,[8 11 12] and patterns of alcohol damage within groups found to depend on more than the total amount consumed.[13] Nevertheless, virtually everybody who studies alcohol problems is agreed that the more alcohol a group consumes the more alcohol-associated damage will result. This important idea (the details of which will be discussed in the next chapter), which has probably changed thinking on alcohol problems more than any other, has led to proposals that the answer to alcohol problems lies less with health and social workers and more with politicians.[14]

Costs and benefits of alcohol

In these days of financial stringency, when an issue becomes a political one a cost-benefit analysis is called for. The aim seems to be to convert every plus and minus to one measure—money—and then hope that the best policy will become clear. This is a difficult exercise for alcohol because the forms of damage are so diverse, the data are weak, and both costs and particularly benefits are hard to measure in money terms.

Cost-benefit analyses of alcohol tend to concentrate on costs. Most people in Britain drink (as opposed, for example, to Ireland, the United States, and Scandinavia, where about 20-40% of the population does not drink) and presumably are aware of the benefits. Those people who drink a little live longer than those who do not drink at all.[15 16] Whether this means there is benefit to be had from moderate drinking or whether those people who do not drink at all are odd in some way is not entirely clear, but some researchers believe that moderate drinking protects against heart disease.[16 17]

Benefits to individuals may be hard to define, but hard figures can be put on the benefits to the British economy. In 1979 terms Britain spent £9000m on alcohol—8% of all consumer outlay.[18] The drink trade provides about 700 000 jobs, the Government raises £3500m in revenue from alcohol, and a balance of trade surplus of £500m results from alcohol.[18] With alcohol providing so much revenue, jobs, and exports, the Government is understandably unwilling to take any political action to limit consumption.

Yet the costs of alcohol are not only a formidable amount of suffering, but also very real economic ones incurred through treatment programmes, social services, lost productivity, damage due to accidents, and policing and legal costs. (These activities too employ many people, a cynic might observe.) A DHSS study group added up these costs—necessarily making some bold guesses in the process—and came up with a total annual cost for 1977-78 of £650m.[19] And this, as the authors explain and the Office of Health Economics agrees,[18] is a conservative estimate that does not attempt to put a figure on suffering. An American Government estimate of the community cost of alcohol was $43 billion in 1975[20]—about £25 000-£30 000m in

1981 terms.[18] An Institute of Medicine study group has suggested that even these figures were an underestimate, and it thinks a more likely figure for 1978 was $60 billion.[21]

Human costs

Whatever the exact economic cost, the human costs of alcohol abuse are enormous. Estimating the number of people dependent on alcohol is difficult: the two main problems are defining what constitutes dependence and discovering how much people drink. One San Francisco study showed that a strict definition of alcoholism produced a prevalence rate of three per 1000, while criteria that included any drinking problem past or present gave a prevalence rate of 272 per 1000.[21] Clearly, where the epidemiologist draws his line makes a big difference. Generalising from figures obtained in one group in one area to produce figures as to how many alcoholics or problem drinkers there are in Britain is also unreliable. Consequently, estimates of the number of alcohol-dependent people in England and Wales vary from 70 000 to 240 000 and those for the number of problem drinkers from 500 000 to 1 300 000.[18]

Adding up deaths caused by alcohol is also difficult. Alcohol plays a prominent part not only in deaths from cirrhosis, accidents, and suicide but also in some deaths from cardiovascular, infective, respiratory, and gastrointestinal conditions. Alcohol abuse probably also contributes to the perinatal mortality rate and the incidence of malformations.[22] The Office of Health Economics estimates that alcohol causes about 5-10 000 premature deaths annually in Britain.[18]

But unlike cigarette smoking, alcohol abuse contributes much more to morbidity than mortality. To know the number of hangovers a year in Britain and how many people work below capacity because of alcohol problems would be fascinating, but these figures are not available. The DHSS study group, however, estimated that sickness absences from work due to alcohol cost about £200m annually in 1977-78.[18] About 70 000 individuals were found guilty of drunkenness on roughly 110 000 occasions in 1980.[17] Finally, alcohol misuse is associated with crime, mental illness, and violence in ways that are hard to explain or measure.

What kind of response?

So what kind of response can be made to this tide of problems, all of which have been increasing for the last three decades? The traditional response has been to try to help the individuals damaged by alcohol rather than prevent the problem at source (although precedents exist of the Government acting to reduce alcohol consumption—for example, in 1751, 1828, and 1914). But there are serious problems with this treatment response.

Firstly, a considerable gap seems to exist between the number of people in the community who have alcohol problems and the number who receive any treatment. One study in south London found a prevalence rate of 3·5% of people with alcohol problems, while in that year only 0·16% had received any treatment for alcohol problems.[23] This difference is due in part to one figure being a prevalence and the other an incidence; also not all of the problems concerned in the prevalence study would need or deserve treatment. Nevertheless, many people who have problems do not receive any treatment. Studies in general practice have supported this finding.[24] These "unknown problem drinkers" raise serious logistic problems for the treatment agencies. As it is the agencies in Britain are overstretched and underfunded.[26] If they were suddenly asked to treat thousands more patients they would not be able to cope —as they could not when a Health Education Council campaign in north-east England encouraged people with drinking problems to come forward for treatment. Many came forward and swamped the available services.

Secondly, doubts exist whether treatment makes much difference to outcome.[27] Martin Plant, somebody who has spent a long time researching the use and misuse of alcohol, said to me: "Whatever kind of drug addiction you consider treatment doesn't seem to matter much—whatever the treatment a third get better, a third stay the same, and a third get worse." Edwards's well-known study presents some support for this generalisation[28]: 50 alcohol-dependent men treated intensively with all the facilities of an alcohol unit did just as well (or badly) after one year as a control group simply given a solemn warning. One of the main conclusions from a large review of outcome studies was that it was easier for incorrect treatments to retard recovery than for proper ones to hasten it.[29]

In some ways the results of these studies are encouraging. They might be taken as meaning that a general practitioner could do a great deal to help patients with alcohol problems in a short time and with limited resources. Russell et al have shown that general practitioners effectively help patients stop smoking,[30] and perhaps a similar study for alcohol patterns would give equally encouraging results. At the moment general practitioners seem to be pessimistic about the results of treating people with alcohol problems.[31] This pessimism about outcome, rather than because general practitioners are not detecting patients with alcohol problems, may be the reason why general practice is making so little impact on the current tide of alcohol problems.

Another way of helping problem drinkers is at work, and this has become popular in the United States.[32] The advantages are that problems can be detected at an early stage and that both employees and employers are strongly motivated to co-operate when livelihoods are at stake. Some impressive treatment results have been seen in some industries in the United States,[32] but British companies have been slow to develop alcohol programmes, partly because of traditional British inertia and partly because unions have been worried that the programmes may deteriorate into devices for sacking employees with drink problems. The Government, however, believes that work-based treatment programmes will be important and gave a considerable boost to the recent booklet produced jointly by the Health and Safety Executive, Health Departments, and Department of Employment, The Problem Drinker at Work.[33] How much this is real committment and how much just a desire to be seen to be doing something about alcohol problems will become clearer with time.

Most of these treatment programmes are aimed at drinkers who have not yet damaged themselves irreversibly. The Health Service is still left to treat patients with severe physical disease and trauma resulting from alcohol abuse, and the social services are left to pick up the pieces of families, marriages, and lives wrecked by drink. Some of these disillusioned and overworked people are the ones who argue most strongly for a comprehensive programme of prevention.

Prevention predictably better than cure

Education about alcohol problems is the least painful form of prevention, and yet there is little evidence that it can lessen morbidity or mortality. Finding an example of an educational campaign that has worked is hard. But then any one campaign cannot be expected to have much effect; few campaigns have been well evaluated; and most of the campaigns waged so far in Britain have started with limited resources and confused aims. Participants have disagreed over whom the campaigns should aim at and what message they should deliver.

Dissatisfaction with treatment and education programmes has led many to suggest political strategies for prevention. Those suggested include raising the real price of alcohol, banning advertising, changing the licensing laws, reducing the number of outlets for alcohol, and increasing the penalties for drunken driving and similar offences. Like most political strategies these threaten vested interests and promote fierce controversy about both the morality and the effectiveness of such moves. A

Sunday Times[34] poll last December showed that although most of the population would favour tougher sentences for drunken driving they would also oppose large increases in the price of alcohol.

Alcohol research

One last theme I want to develop in this overture to a series of articles on alcohol is that alcohol research is underfunded. The changes in thinking about alcohol problems have resulted from what in many ways has been only the most preliminary research. Reviews of alcohol studies—particularly epidemiological studies, which have produced rich rewards—always mention the inadequacy of the data. Britain and even the United States have relatively few alcohol researchers, and the Institute of Medicine in the US has produced figures (table) showing how little is spent on alcohol research compared with the costs incurred by alcohol abuse. Similar figures do not exist for

Amount spend on research into various problems in relation to the economic cost of the problem in the United States

Problem	Estimate of research expenditure in 1978 ($m)	Estimate of economic cost in 1975 ($000m)	Research dollars per thousand dollars of cost
Alcohol abuse	16	43	0·4
Cancer	627	19	30
Heart and vascular disease	284	46	6
Respiratory disease	69	19	4

Source: Institute of Medicine.[31]

Britain, but there is every reason to suppose that they would show a similar pattern. More money does not, of course, automatically mean more effective research, but money is essential and these American figures provide a strong argument for increasing financial support to alcohol research.

References

[1] Anonymous. Booze, Bach, and the big bang. World Medicine 1980;13 December:89.
[2] Special Committee of the Royal College of Psychiatrists. Alcohol and Alcoholism. London: Tavistock Publications, 1979.
[3] Finnish Foundation for Alcohol Studies and World Health Organisation Regional Office for Europe. International statistics on alcohol beverages: production, trade and consumption 1950-1972. Helsinki: Finnish Foundation for Alcohol Studies, 1977.
[4] World Health Organisation Expert Committee. Problems related to alcohol consumption. Geneva: WHO, 1979.
[5] Department of Health and Social Security Advisory Committee on Alcoholism. Report on prevention. London: HMSO, 1978.
[6] House of Commons Expenditure Committee. Report on preventive medicine. London: HMSO, 1977.
[7] Dean M. Can the Government put Britain on the wagon? Guardian 1981; 18 February:9.
[8] de Lint L. The frequency distribution of alcohol consumption: an overview. In: Davies DL, ed. The Ledermann curve. London: Alcohol Education Centre, 1977.
[9] Saunders WM, Kershaw PW. Spontaneous remission from alcoholism—a community study. Br J Addict 1979;74:251-65.
[10] Ledermann S. Alcool, alcoolisme, alcoolisation. Paris: Presses Universitaires de France, 1956.
[11] Miller EH, Agnew N. The Ledermann model of alcohol consumption. Quarterly Journal of Studies on Alcohol 1974;35:877-98.
[12] Duffy J. Estimating the proportion of heavy drinkers. In: Davies DL, ed. The Ledermann curve. London: Alcohol Education Centre, 1977.
[13] Plant MA, Pirie F. Self-reported alcohol consumption and alcohol related problems: a study in four Scottish towns. Social Psychiatry 1979;14:65-73.
[14] Kendell RE. Alcoholism: a medical or a political problem? Br Med J 1979;i:367-71.

[15] Marmot MG, Rose G, Shipley MJ, Thomas BJ. Alcohol and mortality: a U-shaped curve. *Lancet* 1981;i:580-3.

[16] Klatsky AL, Friedman MD, Siegelaub MS. Alcohol and mortality: a 10-year Kaiser-Permanente experience. *Ann Intern Med* 1981;**95**:139-45.

[17] Kozararevic DJ, McGee D, Vojvodic N, *et al*. Frequency of alcohol consumption and morbidity and mortality: the Yugoslavia cardiovascular disease study. *Lancet* 1980;i:613-6.

[18] Office of Health Economics. *Alcohol: reducing the harm*. London: OHE, 1981.

[19] Holtermann S, Burchell A. *The costs of alcohol abuse*. Department of Health and Social Security, 1981.

[20] Berry RE, Boland JP, Smart CN, Kanak JR. *The economic costs of alcohol abuse—1975*. Washington: National Institute on Alcohol Abuse and Alcoholism, 1977.

[21] Institute of Medicine. *Alcoholism and related problems: opportunities for research*. Washington: National Academy of Sciences, 1980.

[22] Rosett HL. The effects of alcohol on the fetus and offspring. In: Kalant OJ, ed. *Alcohol and drug problems in women*. New York and London: Plenum Press, 1980.

[23] Clarke W. Operational definition of drinking problems and associated prevalence rates. *Quarterly Journal of Studies on Alcohol* 1966;**27**:648-68.

[24] Cartwright AKJ, Shaw SJ, Spratley TA. *Designing a comprehensive community response to problems of alcohol abuse*. London: Department of Health and Social Security, 1975.

[25] Wilkins RH. *The hidden alcoholic in general practice*. London: Elek Science, 1974.

[26] Federation of Alcoholic Rehabilitation Establishments Working Party at the House of Commons. *Community Services for Alcoholics*. London: FARE, 1979.

[27] Clare AW. How good is treatment? In: Edwards G, Grant M, eds. *Alcoholism: new knowledge and new responses*. London: Croom Helm, 1977.

[28] Edwards G, Orford J. Alcoholism: a controlled trial of treatment and advice. *J Stud Alcohol* 1977;**38**:1004-31.

[29] Emrick CD. A review of psychologically orientated treatment of alcoholism. II. The relative effectiveness of treatment versus no treatment. *J Stud Alcohol* 1975;**36**:88-109.

[30] Russell MAH, Wilson C, Taylor C, Baker CD. Effect of general practitioners' advice against smoking. *Br Med J* 1979;ii:231-5.

[31] Rathod NH. Perception of alcoholism. In: Madden JS, Walker R, Kenyon WH, eds. *Aspects of alcohol and drug dependence*. London: Pitman Medical, 1980.

[32] Hore BD, Plant MA, eds. *Alcohol problems in employment*. London: Croom Helm, 1981.

[33] Health and Safety Executive, the Health Departments, and the Department of Employment. *The problem drinker at work*. London: HMSO, 1981.

[34] Lipsey D. Random B-tests backed. *Sunday Times* 1980;28 December:1.

THE RELATION BETWEEN CONSUMPTION AND DAMAGE

The centrepiece of the alcohol debate for the last two decades has been how the amount of alcohol a society consumes is related to alcohol-associated damage in that society. The initial argument was whether the two were related at all, but now the issues are more how exactly they are related, how they are related in subgroups of the society, and what determines consumption.

Achievements and failure of Sully Ledermann

The idea that alcohol consumption and damage are related in a society has its origin in the work of Sully Ledermann.[1] The mathematical details of his 30-year-old work, which was essentially theoretical, have been severely criticised, but from the ashes of his theory has risen a formidable phoenix. Ledermann made two assertions: firstly, that in a homogeneous population the distribution of alcohol consumption is a logarithmic normal curve (fig 1); and, secondly, that the number of people who drink a certain amount can be calculated if the average consumption is known. Few people interested in alcohol understand the mathematical details of Ledermann's theory just as few understand the criticisms made by Miller and Agnew,[2] Duffy,[3] and Skog.[4] But they do understand the limitations of data gathered by surveys[5] and that many graphs showing the distribution of consumption produced since Ledermann's time are not exactly log normal.[6] People, particularly those who drink heavily, underreport how much they drink in surveys. Nevertheless, the curves produced in various surveys, although not exactly log normal, are similar and are *always* skewed and unimodal.

Empirical evidence

The evidence that consumption and damage are related depends less on theory and more on empirical evidence. Because of tax and excise many countries—including Britain—have good records of national alcohol consumption (they do not record homemade alcohol, but in most countries this is only a small part of total consumption). Some also have systems of death certification going back over 100 years. Putting together the figures for consumption and damage produces striking correlations that convince most people of the link between consumption and damage.

Table I gives figures for consumption and alcoholic deaths in Britain for quinquennia from 1885 to 1934[7]: the correlation is clear. As Spring and Buss[8] have described, Britain has had several waves of increased alcohol consumption in the past 300 years—and so far the present rise is small compared with those of the 1750s and 1870s. It is tempting but no doubt an oversimplification to point out that this 120-year cycle will give us our

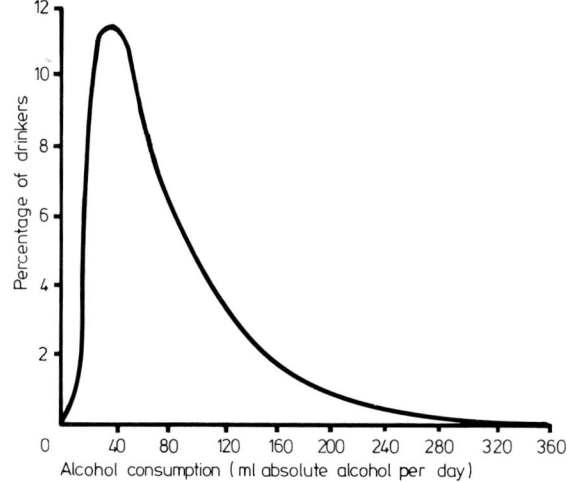

FIG 1—Hypothetical curve proposed by Ledermann that shows alcohol consumption in a homogenous population to be distributed in a logarithmic normal manner.

next peak in 1990. Professor R Kendell, chairman of the World Health Organisation Expert Committee on problems related to alcohol consumption, wonders if there is a cycle whereby one or two generations learn to drink heavily, the next then react to the increased damage with controlling measures, but then as the subsequent generations forget the damage caused by alcohol they begin to drink more and start the cycle again.

More recent evidence—from both England and Wales (table II)[7] and Finland (table III)[9 10]—links consumption not only with alcoholic deaths (as always the most easily measured of events) but also with convictions for drunkenness, hospital admissions for alcoholism, drunken driving, alcohol-related accidents, and crimes of assault. Comparing alcohol consumption

TABLE I—*Average annual alcohol consumption per caput and average annual alcohol-related mortality per million population: United Kingdom, 1885-1934, by quinquennium*

Quinquennium	Consumption in litres of proof spirit	Deaths certified as due to cirrhosis, delirium tremens, or chronic alcoholism
1885–9	17·3	154
1890–4	18·2	168
1895–9	19·1	182
1900–4	18·6	193
1905–9	16·4	156
1910–14	15·5	131
1915–19	10·5	81
1920–4	10·5	59
1925–9	9·1	55
1930–4	7·3	42

Source: Royal College of Psychiatrists Special Committee.[7]

The relation between consumption and damage

TABLE II—*Alcohol consumption, convictions for public drunkenness, cirrhosis deaths, and alcohol-related hospital admissions: England and Wales, 1950-76*

Year	Annual per caput consumption of persons aged 15 and over in litres 100% ethanol	Convictions for public drunkenness per 10 000 population aged 15 years and over	Cirrhosis deaths with and without mention of alcohol per million population	Hospital admissions with primary diagnosis of alcoholism or alcoholic psychosis
1950	5·2	14·0	23	
1951	5·3	15·8	25	512
1952	5·3	15·8	26	668
1953	5·1	15·7	26	775
1954	5·2	15·5	26	799
1955	5·3	15·8	26	1 053
1956	5·3	17·4	26	1 385
1957	5·3	19·3	27	1 535
1958	5·3	18·7	26	1 595
1959	5·6	18·6	27	2 044
1960	5·8	19·3	28	2 479
1961	6·2	21·0	30	
1962	6·1	23·3	28	
1963	6·2	22·8	28	
1964	6·5	21·0	28	5 423
1965	6·5	19·8	29	5 774
1966	6·5	19·0	29	6 088
1967	6·7	20·3	28	6 232
1968	7·0	21·2	30	6 391
1969	7·0	21·2	32	6 689
1970	7·3	21·6	28	8 091
1971	7·7	22·9	32	9 230
1972	7·7	23·7	34	10 167
1973	7·9	25·9	37	11 565
1974	8·9	26·8	36	12 495
1975	9·4	27·0	37	12 751
1976	9·7	28·0		

Source: Royal College of Psychiatrists Special Committee.[7]

TABLE III—*Alcohol consumption per caput, arrests for drunkenness, crimes of assault and battery, cases of drunken driving, alcohol-related traffic accidents, deaths from liver cirrhosis, and deaths from alcohol poisoning, per 100 000 population: Finland, 1950-75*

Year	Consumption in litres of 100% ethanol	Arrests for drunkenness	Crimes of assault and battery	Cases of drunken driving	Alcohol-related road traffic accidents	Deaths from liver cirrhosis	Deaths from alcohol poisoning
1950	1·73	3668	148		20		
1951	1·79	3349	148	37	21	2·3	2·2
1952	1·87	3387	145	50	25	2·5	2·5
1953	1·85	3222	139	50	24	2·4	2·5
1954	1·88	3030	142	46	25	3·2	2·1
1955	1·97	3070	133	43	25	3·3	2·5
1956	1·83	2927	123	49	24	3·0	2·8
1957	1·72	2923	121	49	23	3·5	3·1
1958	1·62	2763	119	58	23	3·6	3·0
1959	1·72	2947	127	75	27	3·2	2·7
1960	1·85	2964	125	96	28	3·3	2·4
1961	2·01	3157	126	116	35	3·5	2·9
1962	2·11	2933	125	119	40	3·4	2·9
1963	2·17	3049	120	128	42	3·5	2·4
1964	2·21	2916	119	135	48	3·5	2·7
1965	2·35	3029	126	144	51	3·4	3·0
1966	2·49	3157	131	152	51	3·2	3·0
1967	2·64	3337	139	154	46	3·2	4·8
1968	2·88	3185	155	147	45	3·6	5·2
1969	4·21	2966	212	178	53	4·1	4·3
1970	4·30	3722	237	197	59	4·2	4·6
1971	4·72	4415	251	215	64	4·1	4·9
1972	5·10	4421	265	243	70	4·3	5·0
1973	5·60	4920	279	289	78	4·5	3·7
1974	6·45	6098	289	350	77	5·4	5·5
1975	6·19	5842	277	379	75	6·3	4·3

Source: Österberg E.[9][10]

and deaths from cirrhosis in various countries (fig 2) provides further evidence of the link between consumption and damage. Factors other than consumption—for instance, pattern of drinking—also determine damage but consumption and damage are clearly linked. Indeed, many swallow part of Ledermann's theory and suggest that an increase in consumption will produce

a disproportionate increase in damage. Survey evidence also supports this belief: an increase in consumption of a half between 1965 and 1974 in Camberwell was associated with a threefold increase in those in the highest drinking categories.[11]

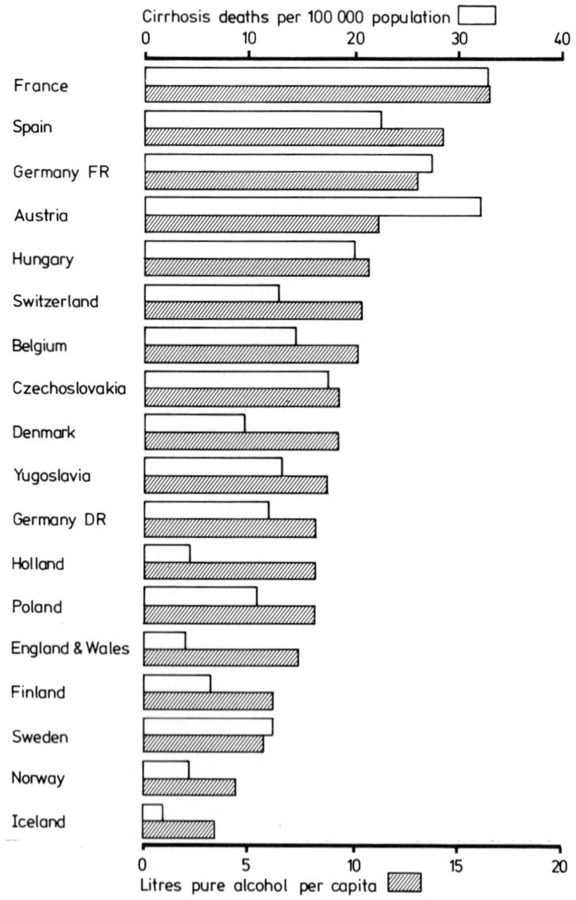

Consumption and damage in subgroups

The general rule that consumption is related to damage continues to apply in smaller groups, but the pattern is not so neat. Martin Plant in his work with Fiona Pirie[6] and Suha Kilich[12] has illustrated this with studies carried out in Britain. The first was of four Scottish towns—Inverness, Aberdeen, Glasgow, and Ayr—and, although the towns with the higher consumption had more damage, the study produced examples of exceptions to the general rule. Firstly, supporting the mathematical erosion of Ledermann's formula, the town with the highest average consumption—Inverness—did not have as many heavy heavy drinkers as Glasgow. This was partly explained by Glasgow having the most abstainers. Secondly, small variations in consumption were associated with large variations in problems. For example, average consumption in Inverness was only 49% higher than in Ayr and yet crime rates were more than 1000% higher, hospital admission rates were about 800% higher, and mortality was twice as high. Many factors must be involved to explain these differences, but to anybody who has spent Hogmanay in Inverness they may not come as a great surprise: if most of the alcohol is consumed on the two nights when the boats are in then violence, crime, and accidents are likely to be the result. Consistent heavy drinking each day—as in France—gives high cirrhosis rates, while binge drinking—as in Inverness—leads to more problems associated with drunkenness.

The second study of regional variations in alcohol-related problems in Britain also showed some inconsistencies.[12] In England and Wales alcohol-related mortality, crime, and admissions for alcoholism were all positively correlated and related in turn to unemployment. In Scotland, however, mortality was negatively correlated with the other three measures. Martin Plant and Suha Kilich's conclusion was that this probably reflected both the poor quality of the data and Scottish idiosyncrasies in recording deaths, but it does illustrate the complexities of alcohol epidemiology. Another interesting paradox is that although Scotland has higher rates of alcohol problems than England and Wales alcohol consumption does not appear to be higher.[13] As Kreitman notes: "It has been well

FIG 2—Liver cirrhosis death rates and alcohol consumption in various countries in the mid-1970s (source: Office of Health Economics[14]).

said that the epidemiologist's primary concern with alcoholism is to escape from the field before his reputation is helplessly tarnished."[5]

What influences consumption?

Working out what determines how much a society drinks is easier than working out what determines how much an individual drinks. This superiority of knowledge about societies is another argument used by pragmatists to advance the case for a societal rather than an individual approach to alcohol problems. Genetics, personality, attitudes, beliefs, religion, culture, age, sex, occupation, social class, experience, exposure, and area of residence all determine how much an individual drinks, how he drinks, and how and whether he is damaged by his drinking.[7] No doubt many factors also determine how much a society drinks,[5] but certain controllable factors—price, availability, and advertising—emerge as important.

Figure 3 shows that as the real price of alcohol has fallen over the last 30 years in Britain the amount of alcohol consumed has risen.[14] Other factors have changed too over these years, of course, but looking further back into British history shows that when the price rises consumption invariably falls and vice versa.[8] Table IV shows the strikingly close correlation between consumption, relative price of alcohol, and deaths from cirrhosis in Ontario from 1928 to 1967.[15] Popham et al studied all the data available in various jurisdictions and concluded: "Almost universally relative price was found to be very closely associated with indices of consumption and alcoholism."[15]

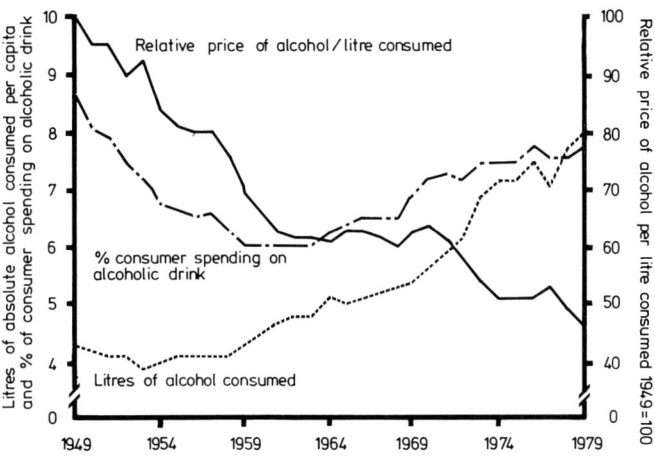

FIG 3—Relative price of alcohol in Britain related to alcohol consumption in 1949-1979 (source: Office of Health Economics[14]).

TABLE IV—*Consumption of alcohol, relative price of alcohol, and deaths from liver cirrhosis: Ontario, 1928-67*

Year	Per caput alcohol consumption in litres of absolute alcohol	Relative price	Deaths from liver cirrhosis per 100 000 population over 20
1928	2·81	0·102	4·4
1931	2·64	0·112	4·0
1934	2·09	0·137	4·2
1937	3·36	0·086	4·5
1940	3·64	0·074	5·0
1943	4·91	0·064	4·8
1946	5·82	0·069	5·4
1949	7·18	0·058	7·2
1952	7·32	0·051	7·7
1955	7·55	0·047	8·8
1958	7·96	0·043	11·0
1961	8·14	0·043	11·6
1964	8·73	0·039	11·9
1967	8·91	0·035	13·2

Source: Popham RE, Schmidt W, de Lint J.[15]

TABLE V—*Cost of beverage, alcohol consumption, and liver cirrhosis mortality in various countries*

Country	Per caput alcohol consumption in litres of absolute alcohol	Relative price	Deaths from liver cirrhosis per 100 000 people over 20
France	24·66	0·016	51·7
Italy..	18·00	0·027	30·5
Portugal	17·57	0·023	48·0
Austria	14·47	0·025	38·5
W Germany	13·63	0·026	29·0
Australia	10·71	0·029	7·8
Czechoslovakia ..	10·27	0·080	14·8
Canada	8·95	0·029	11·6
Belgium	8·42	0·022	14·2
United Kingdom ..	7·66	0·057	4·1
Rep Ireland	7·64	0·092	5·0
Denmark	7·50	0·069	11·6
Netherlands	6·19	0·028	5·7
Finland	4·16	0·117	5·4

Source: Popham RE, Schmidt W, de Lint J.[15]

International comparisons (table V) of relative price and consumption of alcohol provide further evidence.[15] McGuiness[16] in his widely quoted study commissioned by the Scottish Health Education Unit (now group) concluded that price was important but that availability was also very important.

Availability and price have some tendency to vary together, but McGuinness was struck in his analysis by the importance of the number of outlets. Certainly, many people believe that the increased availability of alcohol in supermarkets has contributed to the rise in alcohol problems among women. Licensing hours are one control of availability, and over the years what is probably a disproportionate amount of energy has been devoted to arguments about licensing laws. Evidence on the effects of licensing laws are sparse, and both the Clayson and Errol committees made their recommendations without much hard evidence. Many of the kind of people who inhabit these committees think "civilised drinking" should be encouraged as a way of reducing alcohol damage. By "civilised drinking" they mean the kind of drinking that goes on in a French cafe—with soft drinks, non-alcoholic beverages, and food available, long hours, and a "family atmosphere"—rather than that in a Scottish pub, where furniture, politeness, and women are all at a minimum. This is a subjective rather than objective judgment, and France, we should remember, has a death rate from cirrhosis that is 10 times that of Scotland. "Tavern diversification" in Ontario in 1978 did not lead to any slowing of the increase in consumption over the next five years compared with Manitoba, where there were no changes in the taverns.

Some further historical evidence is available on the influence of licensing. Lloyd George first introduced licensing laws in Britain in 1914 in an attempt to discourage drunkenness among munitions workers. Consumption fell dramatically over the next few years, but the deaths of so many young men—the group who drank the most—may have explained the fall. Also the price was increased at the same time.

In Finland in 1969 a new law intended to relax controls led to a 22% increase in shops selling alcohol, a 32% increase in restaurants with a full licence, opening hours being extended, age limits for sale being reduced, 3000 more cafes selling beer, and 17 000 more shops selling beer. The result was a sudden increase in consumption of 47%.[16] Further evidence from North America showed increased consumption among the young after a lowering of the legal age of purchase.[17] Recent relaxation of the licensing hours in Scotland, however, has not led to any runaway increase in consumption.[13]

Advertising and consumption

The role of advertising in increasing total alcohol consumption is controversial, but little evidence as to its importance is available. The drink trade in Britain spends about £100m a year on advertising, and few people are willing to accept—as the

The relation between consumption and damage

advertisers argue—that this has no effect on total consumption. (The advertisers say that advertising changes only what people drink, not how much.) The example of vodka, which over 20 years has changed from being an almost unknown drink in Britain to one that is now as popular as gin, has convinced many people of the power of advertising. McGuiness in his study concluded that advertising, particularly spirit advertising, did increase total consumption a little, and several independent economists (capable of understanding the complexities of the model) agree with his conclusions. British Columbia introduced a total ban on advertising in 1976 and there were no dramatic changes in alcohol consumption.[17] Interpretation of this is complicated because British Columbians are exposed to the media of both the United States and other Canadian States and the ban did not apply to these media. The same considerations apply to a ban on beer advertising imposed in Manitoba in 1974, when again there was no drop in beer consumption.[20] Nor is much evidence available on the effectiveness of restrictions on the style and content of advertising, but Ogborne and Smart searched for a correlation between the degree of restrictions on alcohol advertising in the 51 States in the US and the consumption of alcohol and did not find one.[19] The importance of advertising remains a moot point, but clearly those concerned to reduce alcohol consumption in Britain should not expend too much of their energy working for an advertising ban.

These studies on the factors affecting consumption have great importance because many people and committees argue that controls on price, availability, and advertising are the best way of dealing with the alcohol problem. But there is a logical step to be made from demonstrating that these factors affect consumption to being sure that policy changes would result in less alcohol-related damage. This will be discussed in the next article—on preventing alcohol problems.

References

1 Ledermann S. *Alcool, alcoolism, alcoolisation*. Paris: Presses Universitaires de France, 1956.

2 Miller EH, Agnew N. The Ledermann model of alcohol consumption. *Quarterly Journal of Studies on Alcohol* 1974;**35**:877-98.

3 Duffy J. Estimating the proportion of heavy drinkers. In: Davies DL, ed. *The Ledermann curve*. London: Alcohol Education Centre, 1977.

4 Skog O-J. On the distribution of alcohol consumption. In: Davies DL, ed. *The Ledermann curve*. London: Alcohol Education Centre, 1977.

5 Kreitman N. Three themes in the epidemiology of alcoholism. In: Edwards G, Grant M, eds. *Alcoholism: new knowledge and new responses*. London: Croom Helm, 1977.

6 Plant MA, Pirie F. Self-reported alcohol consumption and alcohol-related problems: a study in four Scottish towns. *Social Psychiatry* 1979;**14**:65-73.

7 Special Committee of the Royal College of Psychiatrists. *Alcohol and alcoholism*. London: Tavistock Publications, 1979.

8 Spring JA, Buss DH. Three centuries of alcohol in the British diet. *Nature* 1977;**270**:567-72.

9 Osterberg E. *Recorded consumption of alcohol in Finland, 1950-75*. Helsinki: Social Research Institute of Alcohol Studies, 1979.

10 Osterberg E. *Indicators of damage and the development of alcohol conditions in Finland during the years 1950-75*. Paper prepared for an international study of alcohol control experiences, January 1979.

11 Cartwright AKJ, Shaw SJ, Spratley TA. The relationships between per capita consumption, drinking patterns and alcohol-related problems in a population sample, 1965-74. Part 11: implications for alcohol control policy. *Br J Addict* 1978;**73**:247-58.

12 Kilich S, Plant MA. Regional variations in the levels of alcohol-related problems in Britain. *Br J Addict* 1981;**76**:47-62.

13 Wilson P. Drinking habits in the United Kingdom. *Population Trends* 1980;No 22:14-8.

14 Office of Health Economics. *Alcohol: reducing the harm*. London: OHE, 1981.

15 Popham RE, Schmidt W, de Lint L. The prevention of alcoholism: epidemiological studies of the effects of government control measures. *Br J Addict* 1975;**70**:125-44.

16 McGuiness T. *An econometric analysis of total demand for alcoholic beverages in the UK, 1956-75*. Edinburgh: Scottish Health Education Unit, 1979.

17 Moser J. Prevention of alcohol-related problems: developing a broad-spectrum programme. *Br J Addict* 1979;**74**:133-40.

18 Schmidt W, Kornaczewski A. The effect of lowering legal drinking age in Ontario on alcohol-related motor vehicle accidents. In: Israelstram S, Lambert S, eds. *Alcohol, drugs, and traffic safety*. Toronto: Addiction Research Foundation, 1975.

19 Smart RG, Cutler RE. The alcohol advertising ban in British Columbia: problems and effects on beverage consumption. *Br J Addict* 1976;**71**:13-21.

20 Ogborne AC, Smart RG. Will restrictions on alcohol advertising reduce alcohol consumption? *Br J Addict* 1980;**75**:293-6.

PREVENTING ALCOHOL PROBLEMS: A JOB FOR CANUTE?

Journalists reflect tendencies that we all have when they polarise issues and try to force opposite sides into acrimonious and fruitless argument. In this way prevention enthusiasts are sometimes pitted against those who work treating established disorders, but often—and particularly with alcohol problems—the division is false. Prevention and treatment overlap: for instance, is encouraging those who are just beginning to develop problems from drinking to come forward for treatment tertiary prevention or early treatment? This policy has been called both, and it is both. Only a few people in Britain specialise in alcohol problems, and these specialists are adept at moving from prevention to treatment issues. Increasingly, those concerned with treatment use educational techniques associated with prevention, and prevention enthusiasts borrow techniques—for instance, self-monitoring—developed in treatment programmes.[1]

Eclecticism is not just the best policy for responding to alcohol problems, it is the only policy. Alcohol cannot be banished from Britain: though to some people alcohol is the "devil in solution," to most of us life without alcohol is unimaginable. Prohibition does not work, as has been shown not only in the United States but also in Finland and other countries, and while there is alcohol there will be associated damage, and treatment facilities will always be needed. Similarly, health education about alcohol cannot be abandoned on the grounds that it has produced no change in drinking behaviour: any political action to limit alcohol consumption will be unacceptable to the electorate unless an educational campaign has explained why such action is necessary.

If alcohol damage in Britain is to be reduced then treatment, education, and political measures will all be necessary. Nevertheless, when resources are limited—and they always are and always will be limited—then decisions must be made on priorities. This is why a careful consideration of the options is important. Various preventive strategies will be considered in this article, while the next article will examine treatment.

Education on alcohol

Preventive measures may be directed at individuals or they may work by manipulating the environment in which those individuals live. Health education aims at the individual, and in principle few people object to educating people about alcohol problems, whereas many object strongly to political intervention in price, advertising, or licensing. Some, however, worry about the morality of trying to change people's behaviour (they see a distinction between education and propaganda), while others are concerned about the effectiveness of health education.

Then some critics think that health educators may fail because they view their role in too restricted a way. Too often, these critics say, health educators have picked one problem—for example, smoking, alcohol, or obesity—and pushed hard at

individuals, communities, and governments to produce "improvement." But might there not be something tactically mistaken, even obscene, about preaching to a chronically unemployed man living in an inner-city slum about his smoking and drinking? Should not the health educators think more broadly and try to do something about his housing, his unemployment, or whatever? The usual challenge to this idea is that it is Utopian, but the proponents of such broad thinking have an answer. They say that although their approach might be labelled Utopian the more restrictive approach is as doomed as trying to eradicate cholera by asking people to improve their personal hygiene. Better, they say, to try to find ways of achieving what may at the moment look impossible than wasting time on what is bound to be hopeless.

The little hard evidence that is so far available suggests that health education about alcohol problems has not succeeded in reducing those problems. For instance, in 1976 the Scottish Health Education Unit mounted a national campaign on alcoholism. The campaign used television and press advertising, and its main aim was to encourage people with problems to come forward for treatment. An evaluation showed that: more people did come forward for treatment after the campaign; about three-quarters of the adult population were reached by it; those who had been exposed to the campaign did know a little more about alcoholism, but the general level of public knowledge had not significantly increased eight months after the campaign began; and patterns of alcohol consumption had not changed.[2] Repeated evaluations of the Health Education Council campaign in the north east of England have shown no change in drinking behaviour but some small change in attitudes towards drink and drunkenness.[3]

These disappointing results, which are similar to those of other countries, have led health educators to consider more closely what they are trying to achieve and how they can best achieve it. In retrospect, they were naive to expect or even hope for changes in behaviour after such short campaigns. Changes in behaviour are the end of a complicated process whereby first the subject (or victim?) receives and understands the message delivered by the educators; then if he believes the message his attitude may change; and eventually he may change his behaviour. But there are many hurdles at which the health educator may fall.

Firstly, he must reach his audience. The evaluation of the Scottish campaign showed that a high proportion of the population can be reached in a short time by using mass media, and the HEC experience confirms this. But what message should be delivered, and how can it be made intelligible? With anti-smoking education the message is "don't smoke," but what should the message be for alcohol? The Royal College of Psychiatrists' report[4] recommended that to prevent chronic physical damage people should not drink more than four pints of beer, or four doubles of spirits, or one standard-sized bottle of wine a day. Even accepting these as reasonable figures (and

Preventing alcohol problems

some do not) it is a complicated message to transmit in an advertisement, and it is clearly inappropriate for the bulk of the population, who drink much less than that anyway. Also, the limits have been suggested by doctors and are designed to stop an individual developing dependence or cirrhosis of the liver, but social damage may result from consumption of much smaller amounts. Health educators may make a serious mistake if they emphasise the medical consequences of alcohol abuse at the expense of the social consequences. So should the message simply be drink less? That is a vague message and no use to the man who drinks eight pints a day and who feels he is doing well if he cuts down to six.

The Health Education Council has thought about this problem of what message to deliver in relation to its campaign in the north east and this year for the first time has included information on how much people should drink. The advice is "stick to your two or three pints (that's the same as drinking two or three double whiskies) two or three times a week." The message that two pints is the same as two double whiskies is also new for health education, and the HEC has been impressed by the response to these messages from the people of the north east. Whether their impression of a good response will be borne out by evaluation remains to be seen.

An alternative approach is to "fill the information gap" and make people aware of the dangers of alcohol. The Royal College of Psychiatrists recommended that health educators should, "attempt continuously to provide the knowledge needed to inform public debate so that acceptance may be won for the need for a broad range of preventive measures. The fact that alcohol is a drug should be made widely known, the meaning and implications of dependence, the nature and extent of disabilities, the dangers of harm done to others, and the causes of harmful drinking. In particular, the relationship between national per caput consumption and the extent of the country's drinking problems should be brought to public attention."[4] That seems a formidable task and suggests that the college has overestimated both the interest and intelligence of the population and the power of health educators. Explaining the link between consumption and damage to the mass of the population seems a particularly tall order, but an important problem with such grand discussions is that there is no accompanying line of action. A man may be made anxious by alcohol problems but what is he to do? What does it mean to him in his daily life?

The problem of interpretation is another serious one for health educations: too often health education has consisted of middle-class messages (perhaps like the College of Psychiatrists' one) for working-class audiences. The messages delivered, even if well worked out by the campaigners, are often not understood by the audience. Pretesting messages may circumvent this problem. But even if the messages are understood they may not be believed because they conflict with traditional wisdom or because the target individual simultaneously receives contrary information—for instance, that rum means naked ladies and tropical beaches rather than shrivelled livers and broken homes. The final problem is that even if the subject's beliefs and attitudes change he may feel powerless to change his behaviour. Many working-class people feel that they have very little control over their own lives.

Advantages of individual education

Many of these problems of message, comprehension, and confusion about how to act can be overcome if the health education is delivered not by the mass media but by individuals —for example, doctors, nurses, or teachers. Individual educators can tailor the message to suit the subject, can check that he has understood, can deal with questions that arise, can allay associated anxiety, and can suggest an individual course of action. Many health educators, disappointed with the results of mass media campaigns, have come to pin their hopes on individual efforts. The main problem with this, however, is

logistic: where are all these individual educators to come from and how can they be trained? In two months a mass media campaign in Scotland reached about three-quarters of the population, but it would take years for the individual educator to reach the same audience. Again, eclecticism is the answer. The mass media can be used to start the debate and raise the questions, and the individual counsellors can capitalise on the concern created.

General practitioners, community nurses, teachers, and youth workers are the first people who come to mind to "spread the word." Evidence exists, however, that many of these workers are not themselves very clear about drink problems.[5] Much of the alcohol education in schools seems to be of a low standard.[6]

Thus health educators have a tough job before them, and they must work with limited resources. About £5000m is spent annually on the National Health Service in Britain, and yet last year the HEC and the SHEG received between them only £6½m. (Another relevant figure is that about £100m is spent on alcohol advertising in Britain each year.) A further problem is that although health educators may be disillusioned with mass media campaigns their masters—the politicians—are fond of them: they like to be seen to be doing something, and individual educators tend to be invisible.

Considerations like these of the difficulties and limitations of education have led many individuals and committees to examine political measures for combating alcohol problems. Before these are considered, however, two things should be said in defence of health education: firstly, health education has only just started in response to alcohol problems and better results may be achieved in the future: and, secondly, political action will be possible only if the electorate is informed of the issues in the alcohol debate.

Political prevention

Most alcohol researchers, but not all, agree that if the price of alcohol is raised by taxation then consumption will fall and with it alcohol-associated damage. The convincing evidence for the close correlation between price, consumption, and damage was presented in the last chapter. There are, however, no recent examples of a government raising the real price of alcohol to reduce damage. To some extent it is an article of faith that such an increase would reduce damage (although the Polish Government has among other political actions raised the price of alcohol with the aim of reducing consumption. The complex problems of Polish alcohol policy are discussed in a later chapter.)

Various problems present themselves when a policy of increased taxation is suggested. The first is that a myth persists that a policy encouraging consumption of beer relative to that of spirits and wine will lessen damage as beer is inherently less harmful. There is, however, no evidence to suggest that the same amount of alcohol taken as beer is less dangerous than that taken as wine or spirits and a great deal to suggest that it is just as dangerous[7] (although the severity of hangover does, of course, vary with the beverage). The corollary to this message is that a logical policy would make all forms of alcohol as expensive as each other in terms of volume of pure alcohol. In Britain the tax on spirits and wine is much higher than that on beer.

A second objection to a policy of increasing the price of alcohol is that it will drive people to produce their own illicit alcohol. Most who have considered the matter think that this would be a severe problem only if the price of alcohol was raised too much, too quickly. A third objection is that such a policy would be ruinous to those who are addicted to alcohol. This argument can be countered on both empirical and theoretical grounds. There is abundant evidence that when alcohol consumption drops death rates from cirrhosis drop quickly. At first this seems peculiar because cirrhosis takes a long time to develop. But it fits with the clinical experience that a patient with severe decompensated cirrhosis can draw back from the brink of death if he stops drinking. This presumably is what happens to explain the immediate fall in death rates from cirrhosis when consumption falls. The theoretical objection to the idea that those addicted to alcohol will be particularly penalised by an increase in price is that, as explained in the first chapter, alcoholics are not a race apart as was once thought, and even people who drink heavily can spontaneously reduce their drinking if conditions change.

A further objection is that the poor will be hit harder than the rich. But in many aspects of life "It's the rich what has the pleasure and the poor what gets the blame," and this is a criticism less of the health policy and more of a society that tolerates such a division in the first place. Moreover, as the policy is a benign one, intended to improve public health, the poor will benefit more, while the rich will still be able to drink themselves to death. But the alcohol researchers are not making the decision anyway—it is for Parliament to decide. And at the moment price increases to limit consumption are unacceptable to the electorate (table).[8] The Government derives a great deal of revenue from alcohol, which it is unwilling to jeopardise, and the drink trade has a powerful lobby and friends in high places.

Public reaction to strategies for reducing damage caused by alcohol

Strategy	Percentage in favour	Percentage against
Tougher sentences for drinking and driving	87	13
Random breath tests	66	34
More Government advertising on the dangers of drink	63	37
Health warning on all cans and bottles of alcohol	55	45
Tougher licensing laws	50	50
Ban on advertising drink on television	46	54
Ban on alcohol sales in supermarkets	37	63
Total ban on advertising	29	70
Large increases in price of alcohol	26	74

Source: MORI *Sunday Times*.[9]

Alternatives to price increases

Any government that really wanted to control alcohol problems would make price maintenance the main plank in its platform, but other measures—some of them politically more acceptable—can help. One possibility is to decrease the availability of alcohol through licensing laws. McGuinness's econometric analysis suggested that if the number of outlets for alcohol in Britain were reduced then consumption would fall.[9] Canadian researchers dispute this finding, and the paper by R E Popham *et al* contains an appealing analogy that suggests that the relationship is unlikely: "Probably no one would expect an increase in the number of television stores to increase the prevalence of television sets. Actually, if there are too few stores some customers simply will be inconvenienced, and if there are too many some stores will go out of business. We think the situation is about the same in the case of alcoholic beverage outlets (at least, within certain limits: the effect of total prohibition or extreme rarity are special cases). On the other hand, just as one would expect sales of television sets to be influenced by their cost, so also this would seem a likely, if not obvious, determinant in the case of alcoholic beverage consumption."[10]

Reducing the number of public houses, limiting opening hours, and raising the minimum age at which people can drink might conceivably reduce consumption, but the licensing trend in Britain is in the opposite direction at the moment and restrictive licensing laws seem unlikely. Now that the voting age is 18 no Government is likely to raise the age at which young people are allowed into public houses to drink. Nevertheless, various bodies—including the Royal College of Psychiatrists[4] and the Government Central Policy Review Staff[11]—have

suggested that licensing laws should not be liberalised any further.

Another policy suggested is that alcohol advertising should be banned or further restricted. Over the last 20 years the anti-smoking lobby has concentrated much of its energy on campaigning for advertising bans, and many imagine that a campaign to reduce the damage caused by alcohol would adopt a similar policy. As discussed in the last chapter, the possible effects of a ban are hard to predict, but McGuinness has suggested that it would lower consumption.[8] The experimental bans in British Columbia[12] and Manitoba,[13] both of which went off at half cock (see last chapter), did not, however, produce any fall in consumption. Similarly, little evidence is available to support the idea that the style of advertising has much effect on consumption.

Does this paucity of scientific evidence on the possible effects of an advertising ban mean that the anti-abuse lobby should play down the battle against advertising? Many would say yes, but other factors have to be considered. Firstly, the evidence is more scarce than weak: the subject is difficult to study and little good work has been done. Secondly, calling for a ban on advertising is probably tactically better than campaigning for price increases: the public has no strong feelings about advertising but is always concerned about its pocket. A campaign against advertising has a symbolic value and is a useful peg on which to hang other messages. Thirdly, any health education on alcohol tends at the moment to be eclipsed by alcohol advertising (figure). Thus experienced "campaigners" may pay more attention to advertising than the evidence seems to justify.

Contrasting messages on alcohol (supplied by Health Education Council).

Finally, policies can be devised that aim at reducing not consumption but damage. One such measure would be random breathalyser tests, and the Government "think tank" report suggested this.[11] Other measures designed to make roads safer for both the sober and the inebriated, such as the compulsory wearing of seat belts, also contribute to lessening alcohol-related damage.

References

1 Grant M. Prevention. In: Grant M, Gwinner P, eds. *Alcoholism in perspective*. London: Croom Helm, 1979.
2 Plant MA, Pirie F, Kreitman N. Evaluation of the Scottish Health Education Unit's 1976 campaign on alcoholism. *Social Psychiatry* 1979; **14**:11-24.
3 Cust G. Health education about alcohol in the Tyne Tees area. In: Madden JS, Walker R, Kenyon WH, eds. *Aspects of alcohol and drug dependence*. Tunbridge Wells: Pitman Medical, 1980.
4 Special Committee of the Royal College of Psychiatrists. *Alcohol and alcoholism*. London: Tavistock Publications, 1979.
5 Rathod NH. Perceptions of alcoholism. In: Madden JS, Walker R, Kenyon WH, eds. *Aspects of alcohol and drug dependence*. Tunbridge Wells: Pitman Medical, 1980.

[6] Cowley J. The implications of an education model: primary prevention through alcohol education. In: Madden JS, Walker R, Kenyon WH. *Aspects of alcohol and drug dependence.* Tunbridge Wells: Pitman Medical, 1980.

[7] Wallgren H. *On the relationship of the consumption of alcoholic beverages to the genesis of alcoholic disorders.* Helsinki: Alkon Keskuslaboratorio, 1970.

[8] McGuinness T. *An econometric analysis of total demand for alcoholic beverages in the UK, 1956-75.* Edinburgh: Scottish Health Education Unit, 1979.

[9] Lipsey D. Random B-tests backed. *Sunday Times* 1981 January 14:1.

[10] Dean M. Can the Government put Britain on the wagon? *Guardian* 1981 February 18:9.

[11] Popham RE, Schmidt W, de Lint J. The prevention of alcoholism: epidemiological studies of the effects of government control measures. *Br J Addict* 1975;**70**:125-44.

[12] Smart RG, Cutler RE. The alcohol advertising ban in British Columbia: problems and effects on beverage consumption. *Br J Addict* 1980;**75**:293-6.

[13] Ogborne AC, Smart RG. Will restrictions on alcohol advertising reduce alcohol consumption? *Br J Addict* 1980;**75**:293-6.

TREATING ALCOHOL PROBLEMS: MAKING ENDS MEET

Tens of thousands of people in Britain and millions around the world must spend some of their time dealing with alcohol problems. Apart from those working in specialist units treating patients dependent on alcohol, there are physicians managing the physical problems produced by alcohol; trauma teams patching up those injured in accidents or violence associated with drinking; general practitioners wrestling with the whole gamut of problems; social workers helping with marriages, families, and careers wrecked by alcohol; voluntary counsellers and Alcoholics Anonymous workers organising aid; policemen dealing with violence, crime, and accidents; judges and lawyers allotting blame and compensating for alcohol-induced damage; Salvation Army members and others, including prison officers, working with vagrant alcoholics; and ordinary people trying to help friends and relatives having problems with alcohol. This list is far from complete, but it serves as a reminder that, although articles on treatment (including this one) usually concentrate on the treatment of those dependent on alcohol, many other kinds of "treatment" are needed for alcohol-associated problems.

Several profound questions have been raised in the last few years about the treatment of alcohol dependency. The most profound is one that cannot be answered with absolute confidence: whether treatment is any more effective than no treatment. Next, researchers have questioned the relative effectiveness of many kinds of treatment: for example, is prolonged, intensive, inpatient treatment necessarily better than short episodes of outpatient treatment? One particularly hot question has been over the aim of treatment: should it be abstinence, the traditional aim, or can those dependent on alcohol be taught to drink in moderation? Finally, apart from questions of aim and efficiency, those responsible for organising treatment services for people with alcohol problems worry about the logistics of the exercise: how can the limited resources ever be stretched to cope with a rising tide of problems.

The "natural history" of alcohol problems

A useful prelude to considering these questions is to look at what happens to alcoholics if they are "left to themselves"—that is, studied in society rather than in relation to a clinic. Wide discrepancies exist, as explained in the first article (26 September, p 835), between the numbers who have alcohol problems and the number who come forward for treatment. Estimates of the number of problem drinkers in England and Wales range between 700 000 and 1 300 000.[1] Yet only about 20 000 National Health Service patients are admitted for the treatment of alcohol dependence each year. Alcoholics Anonymous has about 10 000 members, and Britain has about 30 local councils on alcoholism.[1] Many problem drinkers must cope on their own, and those seen in clinics may be different from those in the community, which is one reason why insights into the "natural history" of problem drinkers are so interesting, but, not surprisingly, such studies are few and far between.

George E Vaillant of Harvard Medical School has reported the preliminary results of a longtitudinal study of 456 inner-Boston 14-year-olds followed up for 35 years from 1940.[2] With data collected over such a long period, during which thinking on alcohol problems has changed dramatically, there must always be worries about the quality of the information and the relevance of the definitions used. Nevertheless, during those 35 years 110 developed four or more of the symptoms of alcohol abuse as defined by the American Psychiatric Association (a staggering proportion—almost a quarter). Of that 110, 49 subsequently achieved at least one year of abstinence and 22 were able to return to social drinking. About a third of the 49 who became abstinent, and nine of the men who returned to social drinking, did so with the aid of professional treatment, and about a third who became abstinent had been helped by Alcoholics Anonymous. Most, however, had "helped themselves," and Vaillant was able to identify various factors that helped the men to return to abstinence.

Firstly, 53% found help by substituting for alcohol food, cannabis, gambling, meditation, three packets of cigarettes a day, or compulsive hobbies. Secondly, 48% developed a medical problem that was instantly made worse by drinking and so reminded them constantly of the need to change their drinking habits. Thirdly, a third were helped by finding "a new love object" or "an unambivalent human relationship." Vaillant has suggested, as have others, that studying these "natural factors" that aid recovery may be a rich subject for research.

Does treatment work?

The more fundamental a question the less likely it is to be asked, but studies such as Vaillant's quoted above and others comparing complicated and intensive treatments with simple ones have led some people to question whether treating patients with alcohol problems is any more effective than leaving them to deal with their own problems. The question cannot be definitively answered, but some evidence is available.

The methodological problems of studying the effectiveness of treatment are formidable. Firstly, what is being treated: no clear definition of who is alcohol dependent exists (or can exist), and very different kinds of patients may be used in studies. Just as the starting point is hard to define so defining what constitutes improvement is difficult. Some studies define abstinence as the aim, whereas others measure success in terms of decreased alcohol consumption, "normal" behaviour, stability of marriage and family, and keeping a job. Furthermore, the length of follow-up is often widely variable, although some evidence exists that the remission rate after six months is a good predictor of remission rates at later dates.[3] A particular problem when comparing treatment with no treatment is that, although they

Treating alcohol problems

may have little evidence proving the effectiveness of their treatments, few treatment agencies understandably would consider turning away those who seek help for their alcohol problems. Thus, although there are many studies of the outcome of treating alcohol dependency, few are of the highest quality. Emrick[4] has completed one of the largest reviews of reports on the outcome of treatment, yet some alcohol researchers think that he was forced to lump together such disparate studies that his overall data may mean little. Nevertheless, his work is widely quoted as not much else is available, and if the limitations are remembered it is useful to consider his results.

He reviewed data from seven studies of alcoholics who received no treatment and compared the results with 17 studies where the patients were given *minimal* treatment. Patients were followed up for at least six months, and of those who were not treated 13% were abstinent and 41% were improved; of those who received some minimal treatment 21% were abstinent and 43% were improved. Emrick calls for caution in interpreting these results, but they do provide further evidence that some alcoholics can stop drinking without any professional help and they suggest that motivated alcoholics can without treatment change their drinking habits as much as those minimally treated. One study reviewed by Emrick was methodologically more sound than most of the others in that it was a randomised controlled trial.[5] Sixty alcoholics randomly received either intensive, conventional inpatient treatment or inpatient treatment where all the formal aspects of the usual treatment were discontinued and the onus for seeking further help was placed on the patient. After one year there was no difference in outcome between the two groups. As Anthony Clare has said, "it remains to be established that minimal forms of treatment are any more effective in modifying alcoholic patterns of drinking than no treatment at all."[3]

Intensity of treatment

Comparing different kinds of treatment is just as difficult as comparing no-treatment with treatment, but much more has been done and slightly firmer conclusions can be reached. Emrick reviewed 384 studies of psychologically orientated treatment and identified only five that showed significant superiority of one treatment over another.[4] On closer examination, however, most of these studies were methodologically flawed in some way, and his final conclusion was that different treatments did not significantly affect long-term outcome. Costello pooled results from 58 studies reporting a one-year follow-up and from 23 reporting a two-year follow-up.[6] The results (table) showed that a quarter to a third

Results of Costello's review[5] of studies of outcome of treatment for alcohol dependence from 1952-72

	1-year follow-up	2-year follow-up
No of studies viewed	58	23
No of patients	11 022	5833
Improved (%)	25	35
Still drinking and having problems (%)	53	43
Dead (%)	1	3
Lost to follow-up (%)	21	19

of problem drinkers were improved, and Costello attempted to identify factors associated with poor and good outcome. His analysis suggested that active, prolonged, intensive, and inpatient treatments were associated with a good outcome, whereas not selecting patients, large numbers in treatment, poorly motivated patients, and meagre resources were associated with a poor outcome. That poor motivation and lack of selection are associated

with a poor outcome is not surprising, but the association between inpatient treatment and good outcome is likely to be an artefact. In the years that Costello studied (1957–72) inpatient treatment was the norm for selected, motivated patients.

Other evidence suggests that inpatient treatment is no better than outpatient treatment. Baekeland et al[7] could find no evidence that one was better than another. They mention in their conclusions how: "Over and over we were impressed with the dominant role the patient as opposed to the kind of treatment used on him played both in his persistence in treatment and his eventual outcome." Edwards and Guthrie conducted a well-controlled trial of inpatient against outpatient treatment and found no significant difference in outcome after six and 12 months.[8]

In an important and influential study Edwards et al took this work further and compared intensive conventional treatment with simply "advice."[9] One hundred married men were studied and randomly allocated to "treatment" or "advice" groups: the two groups were well matched. The treatment group were offered an introduction to Alcoholics Anonymous, calcium cyanamide, and drugs to cover withdrawal; they were seen repeatedly by psychiatrists and social workers. Their wives were also counselled, and if response to outpatient care was poor then the men were offered inpatient care in a specialist unit. In other words, they were offered as good a care as Britain can offer. After three-hour assessments and initial counselling sessions with their wives those in the other group were given advice with their wives still present. They were told that they were alcoholics, that they should aim at complete abstinence, and that the responsibility was theirs. They were not seen again at the clinic. After 12 months there was no significant difference between the two groups in terms of drinking behaviour, subjective ratings, or social adjustment.

The authors warn against drawing nihilistic conclusions from their study, but certainly this study and other evidence suggests that when the number of people with alcohol problems is so large and the services are so limited it may be a wise policy to concentrate on simpler, cheaper forms of treatment.

Behavioural approaches to alcohol problems

Evidence is slowly accumulating, however, that one treatment—behaviour psychotherapy—may be consistently more effective than other treatments.[10-12] Behaviour psychotherapists are less concerned with the mind of the alcoholic and more concerned with his behaviour and environment. They attempt to identify cues to drinking and the consequences of drinking and then modify the patient's drinking by strategies such as providing other ways of responding to the cues that would normally lead to drinking and "rewarding" abstinence and controlled drinking and "punishing" excessive drinking.

Some of the most impressive studies of behaviour psychotherapy for alcoholics have been carried out in California by Sobell and Sobell.[10 11] They used some intriguing techniques: filming the patients when drunk and showing them the film later when they were sober; giving the patients tasks that were impossible and then discussing better ways of coping with failure; asking the patients to drink in a simulated bar and then giving them an electric shock when they gulped or drank too fast; and, finally, identifying the cues to drinking and trying to find other ways of dealing with them—for example, one patient threw out of his home his brother, who had been sponging off him and trying to seduce his wife, and thereafter he had few problems with alcohol.

Sobell and Sobell studied 70 alcoholic men who were randomly assigned to conventional treatment or behaviour psychotherapy. After one and two years those treated with behaviour psychotherapy had done significantly better in terms of many outcome measures, including drinking, emotional adjustment, and occupation. Such treatment, however, is expensive, intensive, and difficult, and it could not possibly be applied to all those in

Britain with alcohol problems. Even when progress is being made with the techniques of treatment the logistic problems remain—indeed, are growing daily worse.

Alcoholics Anonymous

The only treatment agency not so hindered by logistic problems is Alcoholics Anonymous, the most successful self-help group ever in terms of numbers of members, numbers of meetings, and extent of geographical spread. Controlled studies of it effectiveness are not possible, but most people interested in and treating alcohol problems believe that it is highly effective for some individuals. It started in Ohio in 1935, spread to Britain in 1948, and now has over a million members around the world. The achievement of Alcoholics Anonymous has been not only to help many individuals but also to contribute considerably to changing public attitudes towards those with alcohol problems: it played a large part in substituting "alcoholic" for "drunk." But this very success has led to some of the problems with Alcoholics Anonymous, which is unhappy with the erosion of the concept of alcoholism as a disease and the introduction of new ideas like controlled drinking as an aim of treatment.

David Robinson has studied the activities of Alcoholics Anonymous and described them in *Talking Out of Alcoholism*.[13] Talking is at the core of Alcoholics Anonymous, and the alcoholic, who often has great difficulty in recognising his problem and discussing it with others, by "telling his story" at the meetings and listening to the stories of others, comes to cope with his problem. Although Alcoholics Anonymous concentrates on alcohol problems it provides much more: companions, help with other problems, and what in some cases amounts to a whole way of life. Members participate in all kinds of projects and activities and "cope through involvement."

Not everybody, however, reaches sobriety through Alcoholics Anonymous, and many alcoholics would never go near it. Yet clearly it has provided help for a huge number of people with alcohol problems, and without it Britain's problems with alcohol would be very much worse.

Abstinence versus controlled drinking

One particular issue that has generated much heat is whether controlled drinking rather than abstinence is an acceptable aim of treatment.[14] A central tenet of both Jellinek's disease model of alcoholism and of Alcoholic Anonymous's programmes was that alcoholics were powerless against alcohol: the smallest drop of alcohol might be enough to return a dried-out alcoholic to the path of ruin. No hard evidence supported this idea: it was dogma. In 1962 Davies published a paper which showed that some alcoholics at least could return to social drinking without subsequently coming to disaster.[15]

The whole issue, which has simmered discretely in "socio-scientific circles," was thrown into the public arena by the publication of the Rand report in 1976.[16] This large study showed that alcoholics who had returned to social drinking after six months were no more likely to relapse after 18 months than those who were abstaining after six months. The methodology of the report was severely criticised, but on subsequent analysis the important points stand.[17] Indeed, controlled drinking has come to be an accepted aim of treatment, and some studies have shown impressive results.[10 11] Whether programmes that aim at controlled drinking are better than those that aim at abstinence is not clear, and probably there is a place and a need for both.[18]

This is an issue where the internecine argument[19-21] whether concept of the "alcohol dependence syndrome" is useful or not has particular importance. Hodgson[21] has looked at the data of Armor[1] and pointed out that "the degree of dependence" seems to be important in whether patients do better if the treatment aim is abstinence or controlled drinking.

Conclusions on treatment

So how should those responsible for devising policies for dealing with alcohol problems respond to these incomplete and confused reports on treatment? None of the researchers who have tried to compare the outcome of no-treatment and treatment have ever suggested that treating alcohol problems is a waste of time; and closing treatment units is neither politically possible nor intellectually justified. But, as the Special Committee of the Royal College of Psychiatrists pointed out,[22] we should recognise that in Britain in many ways we have only been pretending to mount a treatment response to alcohol problems: many of those with problems never encounter the treatment agencies; and the effectiveness of the agencies has rarely been properly evaluated.

The recommendations of the special committee seem eminently sensible. Skilled help should be available to all those who want and need it, but people should be encouraged to seek help earlier and to recognise that their own efforts in overcoming the problem are crucially important. Priority should be given to developing those treatments which have been proved to work and which can be applied to large numbers of people at low cost. Clearly such a policy will require considerable research to be done in developing new treatments and evaluating those we have.

References

[1] Office of Health Economics. *Alcohol: reducing the harm.* London: OHE, 1981.

[2] Vaillant GE. The doctor's dilemma. In: Edwards G, Grant M, eds. *Alcoholism treatment in transition.* London: Croom Helm, 1980.

[3] Clare AW. How good is treatment? In: Edwards G, Grant M, eds. *Alcoholism: new knowledge and new responses.* London: Croom Helm, 1977.

[4] Emrick CD. A review of psychologically oriented treatments of alcoholism. II. The relative effectiveness of different treatment approaches and the effectiveness of treatment versus no treatment. *J Stud Alcohol* 1975;36: 88-108.

[5] Levinson T, Sereny G. An experimental evaluation of "insight therapy" for the chronic alcoholic. *Canad Psychiatr Ass J* 1969;14:143-6.

[6] Costello RM. Alcoholism treatment and evaluations: in search of methods. II. Collation of two year follow-up studies. *Int J Addict* 1975;10:857-67.

[7] Baekeland F, Lundwall L, Kissin B. Methods for the treatment of chronic alcoholism: a critical appraisal. In: Gibbons RJ, Israel Y, Kalant H, Popham RE, Schmidt W, Smart RG, eds. *Research Advances in alcohol and drug problems.* London: John Wiley and Sons, 1975.

[8] Edwards G, Guthrie S. A controlled trial of inpatient and outpatient treatment of alcohol dependency. *Lancet* 1967;i:555-9.

[9] Edwards G, Orford J, Egert S, et al. Alcoholism: a controlled trial of "treatment" and "advice." *J Stud Alcohol* 1977;38:1004-31.

[10] Sobell MB, Sobell LC. Alcoholics treated by individualised behaviour therapy: one-year treatment outcome. *Behav Res Ther* 1973;11:599-618.

[11] Sobell MB, Sobell LC. Second year treatment outcome of alcoholics treated by individualised behaviour therapy: results. *Behav Res Ther* 1976;14:195-215.

[12] Hodgson R. Behaviour Therapy. In: Edwards G, Grant M, eds. *Alcoholism: new knowledge and new responses.* London: Croom Helm, 1977.

[13] Robinson D. *Talking out of alcoholism.* London: Croom Helm, 1979.

[14] Heather BB. The crisis in the treatment of alcohol abuse. In: Madden JS, Walker R, Kenyon WH, eds. *Aspects of alcohol and drug dependence.* Tunbridge Wells: Pitman Medical, 1980.

[15] Davies DL. Normal drinking by recovered alcohol addicts. *Quarterly Journal of Studies on Alcohol* 1962;23:94-104.

[16] Armor DJ, Polich JM, Stambul HB. *Alcoholism and treatment.* Santa Monica: The Rand Corporation, 1976.

[17] Special Committee of the Royal College of Psychiatrists. *Alcohol and alcoholism.* London: Tavistock Publications, 1979.

[18] Armor DJ. The Rand Reports and the analysis of relapse. In: Edwards G, Grant M, eds. *Alcoholism treatment in transition.* London: Croom Helm, 1980.

[19] Miller WR, Caddy GR. Abstinence and controlled drinking in the treatment of problem drinkers. *J Stud Alcohol* 1977;38:986-1003.

[20] Edwards G, Gross MM. Alcohol dependence: provisional description of a clinical syndrome. *Br Med J* 1976;i:1058-61.

[21] Shaw S. A critique of the concept of the alcohol dependence syndrome. *Br J Addict* 1980;74:339-48.

[22] Hodgson RJ. The alcohol dependence syndrome: a step in the wrong direction. A discussion of Stan Shaw's critique. *Br J Addict* 1980;75: 255-63.

ALCOHOL AND WORK: A PROMISING APPROACH

Worried by the increasing incidence of alcohol problems, the present Conservative Government is enthusiastic about the possibilities of responding to the problems in the workplace. Obviously, a policy that calls on employees and unions to act on their own initiative fits with Conservative philosophy and is preferred by them to intervention by central government in raising the tax on alcohol. But there are sounder reasons than mere philosophical compatibility for encouraging attempts to deal with alcohol problems at work.

As with so many other issues Britain has lagged way behind with this one. Programmes to deal with alcohol problems at work have existed in the United States since 1942,[1] and France,[2] Norway,[3] and Australia[4] have all taken initiatives that have only rarely been taken in Britain. But now, almost 40 years after the Americans, the Government has produced a pamphlet, *The Problem Drinker at Work*,[5] that might prompt employers and unions to action. The pamphlet, like the Government "think tank" report before it,[6] sets out the solid reasons why a response at work is so desirable. Firstly, most people with alcohol problems are employed, and those problems often first become apparent at work. Secondly, certain occupations are known to be associated with an increased prevalence of alcohol problems.[7] Thirdly, the costs to employers incurred through absenteeism, poor performance, lateness, sickness, and accidents are considerable.[8] Fourthly, people whose livelihood is at stake are likely to be strongly motivated to overcome their problems. For all these reasons, much can be expected from responding to alcohol problems at work, and this article will look more closely at the association between work and alcohol problems and at the various strategies available for a response.

Occupation and alcohol problems

Most doctors are aware of the links between occupation and alcohol problems, not least because doctors themselves are one group with a high prevalence of such problems.[9] [10] The evidence for these links comes from several sources, none of them entirely satisfactory. Table I shows mortality from cirrhosis of the liver in various occupations: publicans have a rate 15 times higher than the average and doctors a rate three times higher. We know that today most cirrhosis results from alcohol abuse, and so this is strong circumstantial evidence of how various occupations drink, but we must remember that this is information about dead alcoholics; live ones may be different.

A second source of information is studies of particular occupations: few of these have been controlled, however, and most are impressionistic.[7] The best early study was of 200 brewers in Austria[11]: compared with controls the brewers had a significantly higher rate of liver damage and more were heavy drinkers. One interesting observation made in the study was that

TABLE I—*Mortality from liver cirrhosis in various occupations (England and Wales 1970-2)*

Occupation	Standardised mortality ratio
Publicans, innkeepers	1576
Deck officers, engineering officers, ships' pilots	781
Barmen, barmaids	633
Deck and engine-room ratings, barge and boatmen	628
Fishermen	595
Proprietors and managers in boarding houses and hotels	506
Finance brokers, insurance brokers, financial agents	392
Restaurateurs	385
Lorry drivers' mates, van guards	377
Armed forces (British and overseas)	367
Cooks	354
Shunters, pointsmen	323
Winders, reelers	319
Electrical engineers	319
Authors, journalists, and related workers	314
Medical practitioners	311
Garage proprietors	294
Signalmen and railway-crossing keepers	290
Maids, valets, and related service workers	281
Tobacco preparers and product makers	269
Metallurgists	266

Source: Plant.[7]

most of the brewers did not know of their liver damage. Some 10 years later Plant conducted a controlled study of workers in Edinburgh breweries and distilleries.[12] He found the same significantly higher alcohol consumption and damage in the workers in the drink trade, but there were other, less expected findings. For one thing, when those workers started in the drink trade they were already drinking more heavily than the controls and had poorer work records. Thus the drink trade was attracting those with a tendency towards heavy drinking. Another important finding was that as some workers changed their jobs so they changed their drinking habits: some heavy-drinking workers in the drink trade deliberately changed their jobs to drink less and succeeded in doing so.

Few other studies have been controlled, but Murray conducted one on doctors in Scotland.[13] He showed that annual hospital discharge rates for alcoholism in Scotland were 3·3 times higher among doctors than among controls of social class I. Some argue that drink problems are common among doctors because medicine tends to attract the unstable,[14] and others that it is because medicine is a particularly stressful occupation. Still weaker evidence of the links between occupation and alcohol problems comes from clinical and general population studies.[7] Eight factors have been suggested to explain the links between occupation and alcohol problems (table II). This classification may suggest preventive strategies for limiting alcohol problems in particular occupations.

Costs to industry

The costs of alcohol abuse to industry are many and various, and putting an exact figure on them is obviously difficult.[8] One

TABLE II—*Factors linking occupation and problems with alcohol (taken from Plant[7])*

Factor	Examples of occupations affected
Availability of alcohol	Workers in the drink trade; caterers; business executives
Social pressure to drink	Coal miners; seamen; medical students; journalists
Separation from normal social or sexual relationships	Commercial travellers; seamen; oil-rig workers; service personnel
Freedom from supervision	Company directors; lawyers; general practitioners
Very high or low income	Doctors; the unemployed
Collusion by colleagues	Doctors; workers in the drink trade
Strains, stresses, and hazards	Coal miners; doctors; military personnel; actors; saxophonists
Preselection of high-risk people	Doctors; seamen; workers in the drink trade

set of costs results from absenteeism, sickness, lateness, and reduced performance. A study of patients attending a community-based treatment clinic showed that 98% of those working lost time because of drinking—the average was 86 days a year—and 66% were often late for work.[15] An American study of medical records of 10 000 subjects showed that those who abused alcohol had an absenteeism rate 2·5 times that of controls.[16] One problem that complicates such studies is that sickness certificates—in Britain at least—rarely give alcohol problems as the cause of sickness even when they are the main cause: one study found that only 3% of the sickness certificates of alcohol abusers mentioned alcohol.[17]

Accidents are just as hard to cost. Sometimes one accident caused by alcohol can result in enormous costs: Seamen, who conducted a study of American railroad workers, described how one factor that prompted the study was a rail accident in 1973 that resulted from alcohol abuse and caused $2m of damage.[18] The large American study of medical records found that the accident rate among those who abused alcohol was three times higher than that in the control group.[16] A French study found that 15% of accidents resulting in work stoppage among 20 000 workers were caused by alcohol.[19] Studies from Britain are sadly lacking, and the Robens Report did not even examine alcohol as a cause of industrial accidents.[20]

The study of American railroad workers gave some interesting insights into the day-to-day interaction of alcohol and work.[18] Some 36% of 1300 employees had seen a co-worker drunk on duty in the past year, and 15% had experienced co-workers too drunk or with too severe a hangover to work. Furthermore, 60% said that they worked harder to cover up for a drunk co-worker, and only 14% would report him unless he did serious damage (7% would not report him even if he killed somebody).

Responding to alcohol problems at work

The Alcohol Education Centre, the National Council on Alcoholism, the Scottish Council on Alcoholism, and the Scottish Health Education Group have all tried to encourage British employers and unions to act on alcohol problems at work. Some companies, particularly a few in the drink trade,[21] have responded, but they are still a very small minority. The booklet *The Problem Drinker at Work*, prepared jointly by the Health and Safety Executive, the Health Departments, and the Department of Employment, may stimulate some action. Experience from the United States suggests that much time is needed to encourage organisations to start programmes: of the 1 800 000 corporations in the United States, only about 3000 have programmes.[1]

Programmes usually have three prongs: prevention, case identification, and referral or counselling. Different programmes have different emphases, but certain key points have emerged from the long American experience. Programmes developed in Britain cannot just be carbon copies of American ones because the circumstances are often so different, but much can still be learnt from American experience.

One golden rule seems to be that employers and unions must work together. Everybody stands to gain, but unions may be worried that programmes will deteriorate into mechanisms for firing drunks, whereas managers have sometimes seen such programmes as reflecting weakness.[22] One corollary to this essential of co-operation is that the programme must apply to both blue- and white-collar workers: alcohol problems will be found in all sections of the work force.

Almost all programmes are based on a written policy, and it is important not only that this policy is agreed on in detail but also that it is "highly visible" so that everybody in the company knows that it exists. *The Problem Drinker at Work* gives detailed suggestions on what such a policy should include.[5] It must state that the objective is to help problem drinkers in the interests of health and safety at work, and it must spell out the organisation's intentions regarding confidentiality, job security, sickness benefits, pension rights, disciplinary procedures, and how the system will work.

Preventive measures will include not only education but also policies on drinking in the workplace and, in the case of the drink trade, on providing free drink to employees. A good policy, and one followed in France and Canada, may be to separate completely work and alcohol. The main part of most programmes, however, is the second stage of detecting problem drinkers. This is where responding to alcohol problems at work can really come into its own because one of the earliest signs of a drink problem is likely to be a deteriorating work performance. The earliest American programmes made a mistake: they called on supervisors to report employees whom they thought had a drink problem. The failure of this approach was that people with drink problems could not be identified readily by physical and behavioural symptoms. If this policy is adopted only those employees with relatively severe drink problems will be identified.[1] A much better approach is for supervisors to report all workers whose performance deteriorates, and then for a suitably trained cadre to find out which of them have alcohol problems. American experience suggests that about two-thirds will.[1] Those that do not can be helped as well, however, and most American schemes no longer concentrate just on alcohol: they are now called employee assistance programmes rather than alcohol programmes. In this way those with other problems—mental or marital problems, for instance—are helped, and some of the stigma associated with alcohol problems is removed. The Americans have found also that many of those with drink problems will respond without any formal treatment, but a referral route should exist for those who need it.

The results of work-based programmes

Few of the American programmes have been satisfactorily evaluated.[23] There are formidable difficulties in conducting studies of outcome, which are similar to the difficulties inherent in evaluating any treatment programme (17 October, p 1043). Hore has gone as far as to say that a randomised controlled trial is impossible in such circumstances.[22] Perhaps he is right, but studies where one factory with a programme could be compared with another without are surely possible. Ingenuity should allow some convincing study to be done.

Some evaluations have been carried out, several of them in terms that are familiar to industry—time and money. The New York Transit Authority, for instance, has about 35 000 employees and has been running a programme for many years. A study carried out in the 1960s showed that the saving in relation to sick pay was $1·5m a year, and this was achieved for an expenditure of only $65 000 a year.[24] Early returns from a General Motors programme have shown an 85% reduction in lost man-hours, a 72% reduction in accident and sickness benefits, and a 47% reduction in the number of sick leaves.[1]

Another important measure of effectiveness is "penetration," or the number of people with alcohol problems that a programme reaches.[1] If a programme reaches only one man and then "cures" him it will have an impressive treatment-outcome rate but will be having no real effect if there are hundreds of workers with undetected problems. The American National Council on Alcoholism expects a good programme to reach 1·5-2·0% of its employees a year.[1] The Boston Post Office identified 8% of its employees as having drink problems in five years, while the Union Pacific Railroad identified more than 9% in four years.[1]

These measures of money saved and penetration may or may not convince British employers and unions of the values of such programmes, but there do certainly seem to be strong pragmatic reasons for introducing a programme. William Dunkin of the American National Council on Alcoholism thinks that alcohol programmes will eventually be seen to be as important in industry as safety programmes are today.[1]

References

[1] Dunkin WS. Policies in the United States. In: Hore BD, Plant MA, eds. *Alcohol problems in employment*. London: Croom Helm, 1981.

[2] Godard J. French approaches to alcohol problems in employment. In: Hore BD, Plant MA, eds. *Alcohol problems in employment*. London: Croom Helm, 1981.

[3] Duckert F. Industrial alcohol programmes in Norway. In: Hore BD, Plant MA, eds. *Alcohol problems in employment*. London: Croom Helm, 1981.

[4] Travers DJ. Policies in Australia. In: Hore BD, Plant MA, eds. *Alcohol problems in employment*. London: Croom Helm, 1981.

[5] Health and Safety Executive, the Health Departments, and the Department of Employment. *The problem drinker at work*. London: HMSO, 1981.

[6] Dean M. Can the Government put Britain on the wagon? *Guardian* 1981 February 18:9.

[7] Plant MA. Risk factors in employment. In: Hore BD, Plant MA, eds. *Alcohol problems in employment*. London: Croom Helm, 1981.

[8] Holtermann S, Burchell A. *The costs of alcohol misuse*. London: DHSS, 1981.

[9] Anonymous. Alcohol dependent doctors. *Br Med J* 1979;ii:351-2.

[10] Murray RM. The medical profession. In: Hore BD, Plant MA, eds. *Alcohol problems in employment*. London: Croom Helm, 1981.

[11] Frank H, Heil W, Leodolter. The liver and beer consumption. *MMW* 1967;**109**:892-7.

[12] Plant MA. *Drinking careers; occupations, drinking habits, and drinking problems*. London: Tavistock, 1979.

[13] Murray RM. Psychiatric illness in male doctors and controls: an analysis of Scottish hospitals' "inpatient data." *Br J Psychiatry* 1977;**131**:1-10.

[14] Vaillant GE, Sobowale NC, McArthur C. Some psychological vulnerabilities of physicians. *N Engl J Med* 1972;**287**:372-5.

[15] Edwards G, Fisher MK, Hawker A, Hensman C. Clients of alcoholism information centres. *Br Med J* 1967;iv:346-9.

[16] Observer, Maxwell MA. A study of absenteeism, accidents and sickness payments in problem drinkers in one industry. *Quarterly Journal of Studies on Alcoholism* 1959;**20**:302-12.

[17] Saad ESM, Madden JS. Certificated incapacity and unemployment in alcoholics. *Br J Psychiatry* 1976;**128**:340-5.

[18] Seaman FJ. Problem drinking among American railroad workers. In: Hore BD, Plant MA, eds. *Alcohol problems in employment*. London: Croom Helm, 1981.

[19] Metz B, Marcoux F. Alcoolisation et accidents du travail. *Revue de L'Alcoolisme* 1960;**6**:3.

[20] Committee on Safety and Health at Work. *Report*. London: HMSO, 1972. (Cmnd 5034, Robens Report.)

[21] Blacklaws AF. One company's experience. In: Hore BD, Plant MA, eds. *Alcohol problems in employment*. London: Croom Helm, 1981.

[22] Hore BD. Alcohol and alcoholism: their effect on work and the industrial response. In: Hore BD, Plant MA, eds. *Alcohol problems in employment*. London: Croom Helm, 1981.

[23] Williams RL, Tramantana J. The evaluation of occupational alcoholism programmes. In: Schramm CJ, ed. *Alcoholism and its treatment in industry*. Baltimore and London: Johns Hopkins University Press, 1977.

[24] Von Wiegand RA. Alcoholism in industry (USA). *Br J Addict* 1972;**67**:181-7.

ALCOHOL, WOMEN, AND THE YOUNG: THE SAME OLD PROBLEM?

Those who treat alcoholics have over the last decade observed an increase in the number of women and young people in their units.[1] This has led to the idea that not only is the prevalence of all alcohol problems increasing but that the increase among women and the young may be proportionately steeper. But, as Roberta Ferrence has pointed out, "it is a well known psychological phenomenon that people tend to overestimate the proportion of persons in a group who belong to a visible minority, particularly when their presence is unexpected."[2] So are there more women and young people with alcohol problems, and if there are why should this be so? Moreover, should these groups be placed in a special category when strategies for prevention and treatment are considered?

Women and alcohol

Just as more men in Britain have problems with alcohol compared with 10 years ago, so do more women. Whether, however, the proportionate increase in women is steeper than in men is hard to answer. The epidemiology of alcohol and alcoholism is, as explained before (3 October, p 895), a difficult art, but Shaw has produced evidence from Britain suggesting that alcohol problems are increasing disproportionately among women.[3]

Firstly, convictions for drunkenness have risen faster for women than men. In 1967, 71 167 men and 4377 women were convicted, meaning that women committed 5·8% of all offences. By 1976 convictions for women had risen to 8642 and they committed 8·6% of all offences. Similarly, in 1968 women committed 1·6% of the 18 384 drunken driving offences compared in 1977 with 3·1% of the 45 369 such offences. But the figures for women remain small compared with those for men, and the changes may not necessarily mean that more women are becoming drunk: they may, for example, just mean that policemen are becoming more likely to arrest women.

Shaw also notes that the number of women admitted to hospital with alcohol problems rose from 1043 in 1964 to 3028 in 1975, and that over that time the ratio of men to women changed from 3·9:1 to 2·7:1. Again, this might be something to do with changing admission policies, but Shaw also presents some necessarily rather loose evidence that the ratio of men to women who present to Alcoholics Anonymous or councils on alcoholism has also fallen. Finally, he shows that mortality among women from cirrhosis and other problems attributable to alcohol has also risen, although the ratio of men to women has changed little.

This amounts to convincing evidence that alcohol problems among women are increasing but not that the increase is proportionately greater among women than men. Ferrence reviewed many studies searching for evidence to support this hypothesis, which is called "the convergence hypothesis." From these studies of change in consumption, mortality, morbidity, and drinking offences she concluded that "there was no clear evidence that rates of problem drinking for women and men have converged." She was reviewing mainly American data, of course, and the British experience may be different, as Shaw suggests. So good evidence exists that women, in common with men, are experiencing more alcohol problems, but the evidence that women's problems are increasing faster than men's is less convincing.

Why are women experiencing more alcohol problems?

Nobody can provide a complete explanation of why the prevalence of alcohol problems is increasing in most Western countries. The increase in consumption is obviously vitally important, but why do so many people drink more than is reasonable? When considering why problems are increasing among women there is a temptation to resort to elaborate but unsubstantiated theories: everybody seems to have an axe to grind.

What is certain is that some of the social and economic factors that have been found to be important in determining how much people drink as a whole (3 October, p 895) are especially important with women. For instance, not only have women's average incomes risen but they have risen proportionately faster than men's.[3] Also, between 1968 and 1977 the number of women working rose from 8 814 000 to 10 066 000, whereas the number of men working fell. Thus as the real price of alcohol has fallen the disposable income of women has risen fast, and this is an important factor in determining alcohol consumption. Direct evidence that women's alcohol consumption has risen is hard to come by, but over the past two decades the biggest increases in consumption have been in drinks like sherry, vermouth, table wine, and vodka—drinks more associated with women—rather than in beer, which is traditionally drunk by men. Individual manufacturers of these drinks also have evidence from surveys that it is women who are buying more sherry, vermouth, table wine, and the like.[3]

A whole pot pourri of social factors have made it easier for women to use alcohol. Working, for instance, not only produces money for buying alcohol but also time and opportunity for drinking. Many women work in jobs particularly associated with alcohol problems: in 1978 there were over twice as many women as men working in pubs.[3] There are now more outlets where women can buy and consume alcohol: supermarkets have dramatically increased their sales of alcohol, and wine bars have appeared and prospered. Some suggest that the success of wine bars depends on the fact that it is acceptable for women to drink alone in them. Furthermore, advertisers and producers have recognised the hugeness of the potential market and directed more of their advertising specifically at women.

Alcohol, women and the young

In addition to these economic and social factors there are undoubtedly important psychological factors. Some talk of the increasing stress on women because of the dual pressures of career and home and general confusion over their roles in society, while others talk of women "paying the price of liberation" with increased alcohol problems. Ferrence makes an interesting point when she reminds us how women have before been subjected to "scare tactics" in times of social change: for instance, suffragettes were told that their reproductive systems would wither, and more recently juvenile delinquency and mental breakdown have been blamed on working mothers.[2] Maybe much of the noise about women and alcohol has the same origin.

Reproduction and alcohol

The tendency to "blame" women for their drinking is nowhere more apparent than with alcohol and pregnancy. The idea that alcohol may interfere with reproduction has a long history,[1] but only in the late 1960s did researchers begin to suggest that a particular syndrome might be seen in the offspring of women who drank heavily during pregnancy.[5] Now a large review has been published[6] and the syndrome has been defined.[7] The Fetal Alcohol Study Group of the Research Society on Alcoholism has agreed that for the diagnosis to be made the patient must have signs in each of three categories: growth retardation; lesions in the central nervous system; and at least two of the three characteristic signs of facial dysmorphology. The study group further agreed that a fetus might develop the syndrome if the mother drank more than "five to six drinks on an occasion with at least 45 drinks per month."[8] ("A drink" is about half a pint of beer, a glass of wine, or a single spirit.) Rosett et al[8] have made the next step and shown that if women who do drink heavily reduce their consumption during pregnancy then the outcome is better than in those who do not.

More controversial and difficult to measure is the effect of moderate drinking on reproduction. The Surgeon General in the United States recently advised women not to drink at all during pregnancy,[9] and the Royal College of psychiatrists has now done the same. But some see this as extreme advice. The Surgeon General quoted a study that showed significantly decreased birth weight among some women who drank only three standard drinks a day,[10] and other studies that showed an increase in the rate of spontaneous abortion in women who had as little as two standard drinks a week.[11] [12]

Streissguth et al, however, looked at birth weight and motor development at 8 months and related this to maternal alcohol consumption.[13] They found that the differences in mental and motor scores were little different except at the extremes of consumption—that is, the offspring of mothers who drank heavily had more problems than the offspring of those who drank nothing, but there was little difference between the offspring of those who drank very little or moderately. Thus evidence of harm to babies from moderate maternal alcohol consumption is still only sketchy, and virtually no data are available from Britain. Such data are needed.

Alcohol and the young

Children in most Western societies, whether damaged by alcohol or not as fetuses, come into contact with alcohol very quickly. In 1972 Jahoda and Cramond showed that most of 240 Glaswegian schoolchildren had formed impressions on alcohol before they started school, and 40% of those aged 6 had tried alcohol; most, too, had encountered drunks.[14] Further studies in Scotland,[15] [16] England,[17] and Canada[18] showed that, although preadolescent schoolchildren tended to be rather disapproving of alcohol, many teenagers aged 13-17 drank furtively sometimes and most were drinking before they reached the age when legally allowed into pubs. It seems, too, that as with the population generally teenagers are drinking more.[18]

The inevitable corollary is that the young are also experiencing more damage. Drunkenness seems to be increasing: one study in Ontario high schools showed that 42% of students had been drunk at least once in the previous month and 5.8% had been drunk 10 times or more.[19] In Hawker's study of 7306 English adolescents 16% of boys and 10% of girls had been "very drunk" in the past year.[17]

A still more recent study by Plant et al[20] of 1036 Scottish 15 year olds and 16 year olds showed that many were drinking and many were as a result suffering health and social problems: 70% of the boys and 61% of the girls had at some time been "merry," "a little bit drunk," or "very drunk"; 40% of the boys and 27% of the girls had had an "upset stomach" from drinking; 6% of the boys and 6% of the girls had had a shaky hand the morning after drinking; 18% of the boys and 20% of the girls had disagreed with their parents over drinking; 26% of the boys and 14% of the girls had "spent too much" on drink; and 3% of the boys and 2% of the girls had lost a day's schooling because of drinking. This is a formidable number of consequences from drinking, and it is interesting and disturbing that the differences between boys and girls in both consumption and consequences seem to be narrowing. Although the girls did not consume quite as much as the boys, they suffered almost as many consequences; they also used illicit drugs just as much and even smoked a little more. This is very different from 10 years ago, when girls lagged a long way behind boys in all kinds of drug use. Another disturbing finding was that only 6% of the boys and 4% of the girls had ever been worried about their drinking.

Deciding how many young people are alcoholics is as difficult as deciding how many of any population are alcoholics: variable definitions and different survey methods make most of the figures almost pointless. The proportion of young people being admitted to alcohol units is, however, increasing: in 1980 4% of those presenting for treatment in Ontario were under 21 as opposed to none in 1964.[18] But as with adults there is evidence that many of the young who drink heavily and have problems stop drinking as they become older. One American study[21] showed that whereas 44% of men at college were defined as problem drinkers only 19% were 20 years later. Disturbingly, the prevalence of problem drinking increased among women.

Responding to the alcohol problems of women and the young

Do "new" groups of the population with alcohol problems need new solutions? As with the population as a whole the response must encompass both treatment and prevention. Studies of special treatment programmes for women are few and far between, but Annis and Liban[22] have reviewed many of those that exist. Their conclusions were that there was little evidence that women did worse or better than men and that, as with men, the type of patient rather than the type of treatment was the main determinant of outcome. Studies of the outcome of treating young problem drinkers are even rarer, but one from Austria suggested that those under 21 and between 21 and 30 had fewer relapses than those over 30.[23]

Health education may be directed specifically at women and the young, but there is no evidence that any campaigns have been particularly successful. Such campaigns need to be both mounted and vigorously evaluated. Parental influence seems considerably to affect how the young drink,[18] and health education might be directed at the young via their parents. Political initiatives to respond to the problems might conceivably be directed at particular groups. Licensing laws, for instance, might be used to influence alcohol use among the young. Smart has reviewed evidence showing that areas in North America that have reduced the legal drinking age have experienced more drinking and alcohol-related accidents among the young than those that did not.[18] But no evidence is available to show that raising the age (obviously a difficult thing in Britain where the age of majority is 18) has any beneficial effect. Alcohol advertising to the young in Britain is already curtailed, but little evidence exists to show that this is particularly effective.

The main message that emerges from looking at problems with alcohol among women and the young is that they are not really very different from those among the whole population. More alcohol is being consumed and more problems are resulting in all sections of the population, and strategies for responding to this problem must be much the same for all those sections.

References

1 Special Committee of the Royal College of Psychiatrists. *Alcohol and alcoholism*. London: Tavistock Publications, 1979.
2 Ferrence RG. Sex differences in the prevalence of problem drinking. In: Kalant OJ, ed. *Alcohol and drug problems in women*. New York and London: Plenum Press, 1980.
3 Shaw S. The causes of increasing drinking problems among women. In: Camberwell Council on Alcoholism. *Women and alcohol*. London: Tavistock Publications, 1980.
4 Sclare AB. The fetal alcohol syndrome. In: Camberwell Council on Alcoholism. *Women and alcohol*. London: Tavistock Publications, 1980.
5 Lemoine P, Harousseau H, Borteyru JP, Menuet JC. Children of alcoholic parents: anomalies observed in 127 cases. *Quest Medical* 1968;**25**: 476-82.
6 Clarren SK, Smith DW. The fetal alcohol syndrome. *N Engl J Med* 1978; **298**:1063-7.
7 Rosett HL. A clinical perspective of the fetal alcohol syndrome. *Alcoholism: Clinical and Experimental Research* 1980;**4**:119-22.

8 Rosett HL, Weiner L, Zuckerman B, McKinlay S, Edelin KC. Reduction of alcohol consumption during pregnancy with benefits to the newborn. *Alcoholism: Clinical and Experimental Research* 1980;**4**:178-84.
9 Anonymous. Surgeon General's advisory on alcohol and pregnancy. *FDA Drug Bulletin* 1981;**11**:9-10.
10 Little RE. Moderate alcohol use during pregnancy and decreased infant birth rate. *Am J Public Health* 1977;**67**:1154-6.
11 Kline J, Shrout P, Stein Z, Susser M, Warburton D. Drinking during pregnancy and spontaneous abortion. *Lancet* 1980;ii:176-80.
12 Harlap S, Shiono PH. Alcohol, smoking and incidence of spontaneous abortions in first and second trimester. *Lancet* 1980;ii:173-6.
13 Streissguth AP, Barr HM, Martin DC, Herman CS. Effects of maternal alcohol, nicotine and caffeine use during pregnancy on infant neural and motor development at 8 months. *Alcoholism: Clinical and Experimental Research* 1980;**4**:152-64.
14 Jahoda G, Cramond J. *Children and alcohol*. London: HMSO, 1972.
15 Davies J, Stacey B. *Teenagers and alcohol*. London: HMSO, 1972.
16 Aitken PP. *Ten-to-fourteen-year-olds and alcohol*. London: HMSO, 1978.
17 Hawker A. *Adolescents and alcohol*. London: Edsall and Co, 1978.
18 Smart RG. *The new drinkers: teenage use and abuse of alcohol*. Toronto: Addiction Research Foundation, 1980.
19 Smart RG, Gray G, Bennett C. Predictors of drinking and signs of heavy drinking among high school students. *International Journal of Studies on Addiction* 1978;**13**:1079-94.
20 Plant MA, Peck DF, Stuart R. Self-reported drinking habits and alcohol-related consequences among a cohort of Scottish teenagers. *Br J Addict* 1982;**77**;75-90.
21 Fillmore KM. Drinking and problem drinking in early adulthood and middle age: an exploratory 20-year follow-up study. *Quarterly Journal of Studies on Alcohol* 1974;**35**:819-40.
22 Annis HM, Liban CB. Alcoholism in women: treatment modalities and outcomes. In: Kalant OJ. *Alcohol and drug problems in women*. New York and London: Plenum Press, 1980.
23 Tuchman E. Rehabilitation of alcoholics at Kalksburg (Austria). *Br J Addict* 1965;**61**:59-70.

THE HABITUAL DRUNKEN OFFENDER: EVERYBODY'S FOOL, NOBODY'S FRIEND

Whenever I am approached by a dishevelled alcoholic in the street whatever I do I feel awful. Just ignoring him seems an inhuman response, but quickly giving him 50p and walking on seems little better: surely he needs much more than money, which he will probably spend on drink anyway. But have I got the time, energy, or inclination to take him home, give him a bath and a meal, and talk to him? No, I have not, and nor it seems has our whole society. Sporadic attempts are made to deal with what are now called habitual drunken offenders, but most end in failure. The habitual drunken offender has few friends: George Orwell included him in his famous book[1]; the BBC has recently produced a film and a book about him[2]; but the present Government has little time or money for him. One of his primary problems is administrative: he falls between the two giant stools of the Home Office and the Department of Health and Social Security. Is he "mad" or "bad"? The Government cannot decide and seems content to let him fall into the chasm between the two departments. The story of attempts to deal with the habitual drunken offender over the last 15 years is a sad but revealing one.

Prison is no place for him

The idea that putting habitual drunken offenders repeatedly into prison is an expensive waste of time is not by any means new. For over a century in Britain people have been making this observation: the Habitual Drunkards Act of 1879 suggested that there should be "retreats" for the "reception, control, care, and curative treatment of habitual drunkards."[3] No such retreats ever existed, but the Inebriates Act of 1898 called for the establishment of State or Inebriate Reformatories. Fifteen were established, but they were not much used because the magistrates thought them expensive, and by 1921 they had all closed.[3]

Other countries, however, have tried alternatives to prison for dealing with habitual drunken offenders. Since 1956 Poland has had "sobering-up stations" where a drunk can be taken by a policeman, examined by a doctor, bathed, and put to bed. He leaves the next morning and only if he is readmitted is further action taken, but the Polish problem is more one of sporadic drunkenness than of habitual offending (see later chapter). Czechoslovakia has similar facilities, and so does Russia. Sweden, too, has a detoxification system, the last stage of which is a voluntary labour camp.[3]

As is so often the case, however, it is North America that has led where Britain might follow. In 1958 Pittman and Gordon published an influential book, *The Revolving Door*,[4] that argued persuasively with good data that prisons were inappropriate and treatment centres should be started. Earlier, in 1956, the American Medical Association had decided that alcoholism was a disease, and then two courts in the late 1960s allowed alcoholism as a defence for a charge of drunkenness. Over the next few years the Government called for and agreed to finance committees to set up detoxification programmes. Several States—in fact, 26 by 1976—"decriminalised" drunkenness, which meant that it was no longer an offence. Sometimes, unfortunately, this decriminalisation preceded the setting up of detoxification schemes, which led to chaos.[5]

Many detoxification schemes have now been set up in the United States and Canada and some have been evaluated—mostly in an unrigorous way. The St Louis centre was one of the first to open, and an evaluation was reported in 1970 at an international conference on alcohol and addiction in Cardiff. Half of 160 patients had improved appreciably four months after discharge: 47% in drinking pattern; 49% in health; and 18% in employment. The arrest rate also dropped, from 46% in the three months before admission to 13% in the three months afterwards. A study at the same centre compared two different treatment programmes[6]: 78 controls were detoxified and given 7–10 days' inpatient care, while 177 probands were detoxified and given three to six weeks' inpatient care and aftercare. The results showed benefit for both groups from detoxification but little further benefit from aftercare.

Los Angeles, Washington, Boston, and New York have all now established detoxification programmes and reported on their results. One important report was on the Ontario detoxification scheme[7]: 522 patients admitted for the first time were followed up for six months; the rearrest rate was 53% with a mean of 4·3 arrests per man. The conclusions drawn by the author were pessimistic: this expensive system had not had much influence on arrests for drunkenness, nor had it resulted in good long-term results for abstinence and recovery. He thought that there was a danger of replacing one revolving door with another.

Numbers of habitual drunken offenders

Britain like all Western communities has habitual drunken offenders, but there are problems in describing them and determining how many there are. For one thing homelessness and habitual drunkenness are not the same thing: not all homeless people are habitual drunken offenders, and not all habitual drunken offenders are homeless. Yet they are part of a similar problem, and a solution that concentrates exclusively on the drunkenness or the homelessness may be doomed to failure. Then, ways of viewing these people have changed: just as all people with alcohol problems were at one time thought of as morally weak so habitual drunken offenders were—and often still are—thought of as pathetic or disgusting people who could never escape from their circumstances. But now those who study the problem see them much more as victims of housing and other social policies and believe that given the right chances they may "blossom." Though, as Tony Wilkinson's programme and book showed,[2] some people opt for the homeless, drunken

when one was established in Leeds—as part of a community project. In Edinburgh, however, a detoxification project had by this time been and gone.[3] It was an experimental project set up to determine the feasibility of detoxification centres in Britain and to try to gather evidence on whether such projects were effective. From February 1973 until March 1974 it functioned at the regional poisoning treatment centre, which was in the Edinburgh Royal Infirmary, the main hospital. Then it was moved until its demise in February 1975 to the Andrew Duncan Clinic, an acute psychiatric hospital. Interestingly, the trial was controlled: there were 52 patients who were given a yellow card, which meant that whenever they were picked up by the police they were taken to the detoxification centre. The 49 controls were dealt with in the usual way.

The results showed that a detoxification centre was certainly feasible, although there were many minor problems and the psychiatric hospital seemed to be a better place than the general hospital. Compared with the controls at the end the probands had better accommodation and drinking habits, but only the former reached statistical significance. Some attempt was also made to cost the exercise: the cost per proband during the experimental year was about 20% more than that during the year before enrolment.

life and are not likely to be interested in attempts to rehabilitate them.

How many habitual drunken offenders are there? The 1971 working party on habitual drunken offenders[8] defined habitual as more than three convictions in a year and calculated that about 16% of drunken offenders were convicted two or three times. In 1967 there were 71 167 convictions for drunkenness among men in England and Wales, which meant about 5000 habitual offenders. The prison authorities, however, thought that there were only about 200, and the police that there were even fewer. But the Scottish Home and Health Department study group of 1978 thought that there were about 2000-3000 in Scotland alone.[2] Since 1967 convictions for drunkenness have continued to rise: in 1977 there were 108 871 for men and women in England and Wales.[9] There are probably many more habitual offenders—perhaps nearer to 10 000 than 5000.

British initiatives

In 1971 a Home Office working party produced a report on the habitual drunken offender.[8] Age-old worries about the cost and ineffectiveness of the penal system, concern about increasing convictions for drunkenness, and the optimism and initiatives then prevailing in the United States all helped to inspire the report. It was a rare moment of optimism in thinking on the habitual drunken offender. The working party recommended a response on several levels: it wanted there to be experiments with hostels, half-way houses, information centres, social clubs, councils on alcoholism, and some detoxification centres.

Nothing happened, however, until 1973, when responsibility for the habitual drunken offender was transferred from the Home Office to the DHSS. The DHSS issued a circular calling for the development of the recommendations of the habitual drunken offender working party and saying that it would provide finance. The voluntary sector took up the job, and the idea was that after a few years the public sector would take over. Although he may not have realised it, this was a golden age for the habitual drunken offender: hostels, shop fronts offering help, day centres, and sheltered housing were all being set up piecemeal round the country.

A detoxification centre was not set up in England until 1976,

Nipped in the bud

In 1977 progress was being made with facilities for dealing with the habitual drunken offender: another detoxification centre was set up in Manchester and various other detoxification projects were starting up around the country; also hostels, day centres, housing associations, and the like were establishing themselves. Then in 1979 came the "cuts" and everything began to look vulnerable.

The DHSS announced that the policy of gradually implementing the recommendations of the habitual drunken offender working party and local authorities taking over what the voluntary sector established would be discontinued: the voluntary agencies were to hand over to local authorities immediately. Vigorous protest from those most concerned led to an extension of the policy until 1981, but now it has been discontinued. So far nothing has been lost but there can be no more growth.

But, while the DHSS has turned away from the problem, the Home Office has again become concerned because the prisons are now fuller than ever. The Home Office has no power to set up detoxification centres—because they are a health matter—but it has developed plans for "wet shelters." Those who have been concerned with detoxification centres think that "wet shelters" will be nothing more than cheap police cells: they have little medical cover, and the patients are thrown out after 24 hours. The primary aim of these shelters seems to be not to help the habitual drunken offender but rather to keep him out of the way.

So one decade has seen the rise and fall of grand schemes for dealing with the habitual drunken offender. At the moment things are presumably better than they were 10 years ago in so far as some detoxification projects and many community facilities now exist. But how long will they survive and how can they deal with what are likely to be expanding problems as rising unemployment and rising alcohol consumption take their toll? Is it inevitable that as times get harder then habitual drunken offenders are ignored? Is our society quite incapable of dealing with these chronic problems?

References

[1] Orwell G. *Down and out in Paris and London.* Harmondsworth: Penguin, 1981.
[2] Wilkinson T. *Down and out.* London: Quartet, 1981.

The habitual drunken offender

[3] Hamilton JR, Griffith A, Ritson B, Aitken RCB. *Detoxification of habitual drunken offenders.* Edinburgh: Scottish Home and Health Department, 1978.

[4] Pittman DJ, Gordon CW. *Revolving door: a study of the chronic police case inebriate.* Glencoe: Free Press, 1958.

[5] Dunea G. Return of the hangman. *Br Med J* 1977;i:1069-70.

[6] Pittman DJ, Tate RL. A comparison of two treatment programs for alcoholics. *Quarterly Journal of Studies on Alcohol* 1969;**30**:888-99.

[7] Smart R. The Ontario detoxification system—an evaluation of its effectiveness. In: Madden JS, Walker R, Kenyon WH, eds. *Alcohol and drug dependence. A multidisciplinary approach.* New York: Plenum, 1977: 321-8.

[8] Working Party on Habitual Drunken Offenders. *Report.* London: HMSO, 1971.

[9] Special Committee of the Royal College of Psychiatrists. *Alcohol and Alcoholism.* London: Tavistock Publications, 1979.

POLISH LESSONS ON ALCOHOL POLICY

Within 24 hours of taking over Poland in December 1981 the Military Council of National Salvation imposed a ban on the sale of alcohol. Similarly, in Gdansk in August 1980 at the beginning of the strike in the Lenin shipyards that led eventually to the formation of Solidarity, the independent trade union, the selling of alcohol was banned. It was banned also in all other areas where there were strikes. What was particularly interesting about the total ban imposed during the strikes was that both sides—the regional governments and the strike committees—claimed that they had introduced the bans. This confused the alcohol researchers who had gone to study this "experiment" of prohibition until they looked back at other Polish industrial disputes. More often than not one side had accused the other of being "nothing better than a mob of drunks." Consequently in the modern disputes each side was anxious to show that it was against alcohol abuse and that its policies were inspired by political zeal and not alcohol.

These are the most recent and most dramatic examples of the political importance of alcohol in Poland, but ever since the last century, when landowners were accused of using alcohol to subjugate their serfs, it has had this importance. Just as in Britain, Poland has had waves of increased alcohol consumption associated with increased alcohol-related damage over the last three centuries, and, just as in most Western countries, consumption and damage have been increasing in the last 20 years. Yet, in contrast to the British Government, the Polish Government has paid great attention to alcohol problems. A series of laws relating to the treatment and prevention of alcoholism have been passed since 1956, and since 1957 there has been a government commission on alcohol problems. In 1971 a permanent government commission on alcohol problems, composed of vice-ministers of all the interested ministries, was established. Its job was to "co-ordinate and initiate prevention of alcoholism throughout the country, prepare programmes of prevention of alcoholism and alcohol abuse, and draft appropriate legislation."[1] It was helped by an expert advisory committee, which until recently was headed by a doctor. And with the rise of Solidarity, alcohol became an even more political issue: Solidarity too had policies on alcohol and had also set up its own advisory committee.

Consequently, when it is being argued increasingly in Britain[2][3] and other countries[4] that the answer to the rising tide of alcohol problems lies more with politicians than with health and social workers, there was much in Poland to interest those concerned with alcohol. I went to Poland (in December 1981, leaving four days before martial law was imposed) and met among others the last chairman of the government's expert advisory committee and the man who had organised Solidarity's expert committee. I was also supplied with data by researchers from the alcohol research unit in the Psychoneurological Institute in Warsaw, and with all this information I can tell a story that

has intrinsic interest as well as lessons for those in all countries concerned to limit alcohol problems.

Alcohol and alcohol problems before Solidarity

The appearance of Solidarity divides recent Polish history into two parts[5] not only because of Solidarity's activities but also because of the severe economic problems that played such an important part in Solidarity's formation. This division applies to alcohol policies, and I want first to consider alcohol use and problems in Poland before Solidarity.

Table I shows data on alcohol for Poland from 1956 to 1980[1][6]; it is interesting to compare it with similar data for England and Wales (table II). Alcohol consumption per head during the last 30 years has always been lower in Poland than in England and Wales, but the proportionate increase has been greater. These figures (like all figures) deceive to some extent, however, because a higher percentage of Poles (about 20% as opposed about 5% of Britons) do not drink at all.

Poles drink in quite a different way from the English and the Welsh. Firstly, they drink mostly spirits—mainly vodka. For every year of the last 40 years always more than 60% of all the alcohol drunk in Poland has been in the form of spirits (and as foreign spirits like whisky and cognac are sold by the government

TABLE I—*Alcohol consumption and alcohol-related damage in Poland from 1950 to 1980*

Year	Per caput consumption in litres of 100% alcohol	Deaths from liver cirrhosis per 100 000 population	Admissions to hospital for alcoholic psychosis per 100 000 population	Admissions to sobering-up stations (in 000s)	First admissions to hospital for treatment of alcoholism per 100 000 population	Deaths from alcohol poisoning per 100 000 population
1950	2·96					1·0
1956	3·44		2·3	7·6	2·5	1·0
1960	3·81	3·4	2·0	102·3	7·4	0·4
1961	3·97	3·9	2·3	113·6	8·4	0·7
1962	3·88	4·8	2·3	118·3	9·9	0·9
1963	4·0	5·8	2·5	122·3	9·2	0·9
1964	3·89	5·9	2·0	129·6	9·7	0·9
1965	4·10	6·0	3·2	144·2	10·7	1·2
1966	4·30	6·6	3·6	157·4	11·8	1·4
1967	4·64	7·1	3·8	171·8	11·9	1·4
1968	4·98	7·5	3·6	172·5	10·2	2·0
1969	5·61	8·1	4·2	184·8	11·5	2·1
1970	5·27	8·3	4·7	214·1	13·1	2·0
1971	5·63	9·0	5·1	223·9	13·9	2·3
1972	6·17	9·4	5·9	238·6	14·1	2·4
1973	6·65	9·7	6·5	247·6	15·4	2·6
1974	6·35	9·6	6·1	247·1	16·6	2·5
1975	7·10	10·2	7·2	292·0	16·7	2·7
1976			8·7			
1977	8·3					
1978	8·0		10·5			
1979	8·0		10·1			
1980	8·4		10·7			

Polish lessons on alcohol policy

TABLE II—*Alcohol consumption, convictions for public drunkenness, deaths from cirrhosis, and alcohol-related hospital admissions in England and Wales, 1950-76*

Year	Annual per caput consumption of persons aged 15 and over in litres of 100% ethanol	Convictions for public drunkenness per 10 000 population aged 15 years and over	Deaths from cirrhosis with and without mention of alcohol per million population	Hospital admissions with primary diagnosis of alcoholism or alcoholic psychosis
1950	5·2	14·0	23	
1951	5·3	15·8	25	512
1952	5·3	15·8	26	668
1953	5·1	15·7	26	775
1954	5·2	15·5	26	799
1955	5·3	15·8	26	1 053
1956	5·3	17·4	26	1 385
1957	5·3	19·3	27	1 535
1958	5·3	18·7	26	1 595
1959	5·6	18·6	27	2 044
1960	5·8	19·3	28	2 479
1961	6·2	21·0	30	
1962	6·1	23·3	28	
1963	6·2	22·8	28	
1964	6·5	21·0	28	5 423
1965	6·5	19·8	29	5 774
1966	6·5	19·0	29	6 088
1967	6·7	20·3	28	6 232
1968	7·0	21·2	30	6 391
1969	7·0	21·2	32	6 689
1970	7·3	21·6	28	8 091
1971	7·7	22·9	32	9 230
1972	7·7	23·7	34	10 167
1973	7·9	25·9	37	11 565
1974	8·9	26·8	36	12 495
1975	9·4	27·0	37	12 751
1976	9·7	28·0		

Source: Royal College of Psychiatrists Special Committee[a]

TABLE III—*Pattern of alcoholic consumption in Poland*

Year	Percentage of alcohol consumed as		
	Spirits	Wine	Beer
1938	88·0	1·7	10·3
1950	78·4	3·8	17·8
1951	75·5	5·2	19·3
1952	73·1	6·4	20·5
1953	69·7	6·8	23·5
1954	68·8	8·5	22·7
1955	69·0	9·5	21·5
1956	69·0	10·4	20·6
1957	70·1	11·1	18·8
1958	66·2	12·9	20·9
1959	63·3	15·1	21·6
1960	62·4	14·8	22·8
1961	61·4	16·1	22·5
1962	63·1	15·8	21·1
1963	62·9	14·7	22·4
1964	61·1	15·6	23·3
1965	63·1	14·6	22·3
1966	64·4	13·0	22·6
1967	65·4	12·7	21·9
1968	65·3	12·7	22·0
1969	64·7	13·4	21·9
1970	63·1	13·7	23·2
1971	63·0	13·9	23·1
1972	64·3	13·3	22·4
1973	65·6	12·5	21·9
1974	64·4	13·5	22·1
1975	66·7	13·0	20·3
1976	69·2	14·1	16·7

drunk a little by the time they are 12 and the number of young people seen in alcohol units has been beginning to increase.

Despite these traditional patterns of hard drinking one thing that is different between Britain and Poland is public attitudes on policies to control drinking: in 1976 in response to the question "Do you think something should be done by the State or the society to ensure that people drink less in Poland?" only 4% said no. More than 85% thought yes, and 34% thought something should be done urgently. Most Britons, however, are against the government taking action such as banning advertising and raising prices to reduce alcohol consumption.

Causes of rising consumption

Many factors underlie the increase in consumption of alcohol per head in Poland. The State has considerable powers to influence consumption: spirit production, through the Spirits Industry Enterprises (POLMOS), is a State monopoly, and although the means of producing wine and beer are not State owned, it has considerable power over them. Most of the alcohol consumed in Poland is produced there: imports and exports count for little. The State also controls the number of retail outlets.

But, although the State has this power and although it has since 1956 had a commission to oversee alcohol policy, many competing interests have to be taken into account when making policy. In the '70s about 10% of State revenue came from alcohol and about 40 000 people (0·8% of the industrial work force) were employed in producing it and about 50–70 000 people in retailing it. Even in a centralised economy health factors are by no means the only ones to be considered when policy is being decided.

Between 1950 and 1980 in Poland, as in most other countries, it was price relative to income that seemed to play the main part in determining alcohol consumption per head. (This usually all-important mechanism has broken down in the last year in Poland, as I will describe later.) Between 1950 and 1975 there were nine increases in the price of alcohol, ranging from 12% to 40% and each time leading to a temporary moderation in the increase in consumption. To take a broader perspective, however, the price of alcohol relative to real income (table IV) goes a long way to explaining the consumption pattern. In the early

TABLE IV—*Real wages, living costs, and price of alcohol in Poland in selected years*

	1960	1965	1970	1975
Average real wage index	100·0	107·7	119·5	169·0
Living cost index	100·0	111·3	120·3	135·5
Alcoholic beverages price index ..	100·0	125·2	145·3	184·8

at a much higher price than Polish vodka most of the spirit consumed is vodka) (table III). The Poles, however, drink their vodka neat, and they drink it to get drunk. Even in these hard times I managed to experience true Polish drinking: as the meal appears on the table a glass (it used to be a tumbler) of neat vodka appears with it. Even in the politest circles this is drunk straight down and followed by several more glasses. Within 15 minutes you are expected to be mildly drunk. This does not happen at every meal but at special meals, and each person would normally consume between 0·25 and 0·5 l of vodka. To some extent this traditional pattern of drinking has been eroded by campaigns encouraging sobriety but is still the norm.

Most Poles drink either in their own home or in the home of friends. Only about a third of all drinking goes on in bars or restaurants. Just as in Britain, women drink less and on fewer occasions than men and experience fewer problems, although, again as in Britain, their traditional abstemiousness may be changing. It is illegal to sell alcoholic beverages over 4·5% strength to people under 18. Nevertheless, most children have

'60s, when the price of alcohol increased faster than real wages, consumption remained steady. In the late '60s average real wages began to rise fast and outstripped the rise in the price of alcohol. Accordingly, consumption rose. Indeed, between 1950 and 1970, when consumer expenditure rose from 249·4 billion zlotys to 790·4 billion zlotys, the proportion spent on alcohol rose from 8·5% to 13·2%. Variations in price also explain the small swing away from vodka that occurred in the '60s (table III): wine and beer became slightly cheaper relative to vodka. This trend was reversed when vodka became proportionately cheaper.

Other factors seem to have had only a small influence on consumption. As we are often reminded by alcohol advertisers in Britain, there is no alcohol advertising in Poland as in the rest of the Eastern bloc. It is not illegal; it just does not happen. There are, however, licensing laws and strict rules on places where selling alcohol is not allowed—for example, factories, educational establishments, and sports centres. In theory the number of retail outlets is controlled, but in practice these controls have not been observed and in 1979 there were some 50 000 outlets in Poland.

Rising alcohol-related damage

Against this backcloth of rising consumption an increase in alcohol-related damage would be expected, and the statistics show that this has occurred (table I). The incidence of deaths from cirrhosis almost trebled between 1960 and 1975. First admissions for the treatment of alcoholism per 100 000 of the population more than doubled between 1960 and 1975—of course, reflecting to some extent the increase in facilities. A 1956 law introduced compulsory treatment of alcoholics, but this became less and less practicable—both because sufficient facilities were not available and because compulsory treatment of unwilling patients was proving fruitless. As well as eight specialist alcohol units in Poland in 1976 there were some 431 "temperance outpatient clinics" and a handful of Alcoholics Anonymous groups. Between 1960 and 1976 deaths from alcohol poisoning increased about sevenfold. Furthermore, the Poles keep figures on hospital admissions for alcohol psychosis; indeed, Professor I Wald, the director of the Psychoneurological Institute, believes that in Poland this is the most sensitive indicator of alcohol problems. Between 1960 and 1979 the incidence of such admissions quadrupled.

Another thing that the 1956 alcohol law did was to "decriminalise" drunkenness. Instead, those drunk and "behaving indecently in public" were taken to sobering-up stations, where they were detained for 24 hours, seen by doctors, and then asked to pay. The first station was founded in 1956, and in 1976 there were 35 with 1517 beds. Admissions to these have soared (table I), but much of this is a function of increased availability. Figures were also available on convictions for drunken driving, but changes in the law, changes in the energy with which policemen implemented the law, and the paucity of cars made these unhelpful.

So before Solidarity appeared, despite alcohol always having been an important political issue in Poland and despite the government having had almost complete control over alcohol production and sale and having an interdepartmental committee for deciding policy, alcohol consumption had been increasing, as had alcohol-related problems.

Alcohol initiatives since Solidarity

Solidarity was very concerned about alcohol problems right from the beginning. Indeed, many of its members believed that the Polish Government had used alcohol to suppress the Polish people. They said that the Polish Government had only two concerns: to make as much money as possible out of alcohol and "to keep the society drunk so that it was easy to manage." Three pieces of evidence were brought forward to support that claim: firstly, alcohol was always very freely available in Poland when most other consumer goods were not; secondly, until 1976 there was censorship on information on alcohol and alcohol problems; and, thirdly, the government allowed far more retail outlets to operate than were legally allowed.

As I said at the beginning of this article, prohibition was introduced at the beginning of the strikes in the summer of 1980. Furthermore, the strike committees were very strict about not allowing alcohol to be consumed by the strikers. Once the strikes were over and Solidarity had made its accusations that the government had used alcohol to suppress the people, it and the government began to vie with each other to produce more radical policies to reduce alcohol consumption. In two months the government reduced the number of alcohol outlets from about 50 000 to 30 000. Meanwhile, Solidarity wanted them reduced to 3000. This was clearly ludicrous, and various alcohol experts dissuaded it from such drastic action. It did, however, produce a plan for combating alcohol problems, though some of the points in it were equally ludicrous—one, for instance, was for all people admitted to sobering-up stations to be tested for syphilis. One thing that Solidarity called for and with which the government agreed was for the abolition of "low quality" fruit wine; this was the drink of the young, but "low quality" was not defined and implementing the policy was thus difficult.

The result of all this rhetoric was that people panicked and began to buy up alcohol as fast as they could. Expecting that a severe policy would be introduced, and at a time when everything was beginning to disappear from the shops, people bought whatever they could. It was then that queues for alcohol first appeared.

The breakdown of alcohol policy

In February 1981 General Jaruzelski came to power and brought with him a ten-point plan; one of these was to strengthen the campaign against alcohol abuse. A few days later the government announced that the price of alcohol would soon be increased. The queues became longer. Also at this time alcohol production began to fall because the farmers were refusing to sell their potatoes to the government. Furthermore, the government (perhaps to save its face) decided officially to decrease alcohol production by 20–30%. Eventually in March the price of vodka was increased by 50% and that of wine and beer by 10–20%. But a few days after these increases were announced there were more strikes and prohibition was introduced for another 10 days.

The result of all this panic, confusion, and prohibition was that price was no longer the main determinant of consumption. People were willing to spend anything on the black market and in the shops to get alcohol. Supply rather than price was the crucial factor in determining consumption. Then in the summer alcohol was rationed: people were allowed half a litre of vodka a month. This led to people buying alcohol whether they drank or not, and after further price increases on 1 December a bottle of vodka cost 400 zlotys (there were officially about 60 zlotys to the pound). Yet the average monthly income was only 7000 zlotys.

So in December 1981 Polish people were spending much of their income on alcohol and yet getting only small amounts because so little was available. Were people producing their own alcohol and what was happening to those people dependent on alcohol? Little information was available on arrests for illicit production of alcohol, but several doctors told me that poisons units were having a busy time—less with people drinking methanol but more with alcoholics who had been drinking antifreeze or whatever came to hand. In contrast, the psychiatric units were seeing few people with alcohol problems.

The future and the lessons

What will happen now? With the arrival of martial law maybe alcohol problems will be forgotten, but a new alcohol law was planned for 1982. Among other policies it was going to stop compulsory treatment of alcoholics, give a greater emphasis to prevention, and provide more support for social and voluntary programmes. Solidarity, too, had submitted proposals. The main thrust of these was to decentralise control over problems and allow local communities to make more decisions. Solidarity also wanted to depend more on education and less on manipulation by price as a means of reducing problems. (This is ironic as it is essentially the same policy as the British Conservative Government's; what is radical in one society is square in another.)

What lessons are there for us in Britain? There is much to fascinate the alcohol student, but I have come away with two main lessons. One is the specific one that in certain circumstances trying to control alcohol consumption by manipulating price will not work. The more general lesson is that counteracting alcohol problems by political means may not be quite as easy as it seems it might be to those of us living in a country where such measures are largely ignored.

Polish lessons on alcohol policy

References

[1] Moskalewicz J. *Preliminary inventory of data—Poland*. Warsaw: Psychoneurological Institute, 1980.

[2] Kendell RE. Alcoholism: a medical or a political problem? *Br Med J* 1979;ii:367-71.

[3] Special Committee of the Royal College of Psychiatrists. *Alcohol and alcoholism*. London: Tavistock Publications, 1979.

[4] Moser J. *Prevention of alcohol-related problems: an international review of preventive measures, policies, and programmes*. Toronto: Alcoholism and Drug Addiction Research Foundation, 1980.

[5] Macshane D. *Solidarity: Poland's independent trade union*. Nottingham: Spokesman, 1981.

[6] Wald I, Kulisiewicz T, Morawski J, Bogustawski A. *Raport o problemach polityki w Zakesie alkoholu.* (Report on alcohol policy.) Warsaw: Zwiazków Zawodowych, 1981.

ALCOHOL IN THE THIRD WORLD:
A CHANCE TO AVOID A MISERABLE TRAP

When 17 million children a year die of malnutrition in the Third World[1] and about 12 million cases of malaria are reported each year to the World Health Organisation,[2] the problems caused by alcohol in the Third World may seem relatively unimportant. So they are in relation to these problems, but two factors make alcohol-related questions well worth considering. Firstly, the admittedly poor evidence available suggests that the consumption of alcohol and with it many associated social, health, and economic problems are increasing rapidly in the Third World.[3-5] Secondly, and more crucially, much evidence suggests that many alcohol problems can be prevented by administrative and political measures.[5-7] In other words, if Third World governments wake up to the threat of alcohol problems they may be able to avoid them without huge expenditure of time, money, and effort. Malnutrition and malaria are much less easy to prevent.

The developed world and the WHO undoubtedly have a part to play in helping Third World countries to avoid the misery caused by alcohol that is now seen in abundance in richer countries. The role will not be to preach, patronise, or direct but to make available the large amount of evidence accumulated in developed countries on the causes and the prevention of alcohol problems. WHO has, indeed, been doing this for some time, and next year it will be holding a large international conference on alcohol in the Third World.

Extent of alcohol problems

As might be expected, statistics on alcohol consumption and alcohol problems are often either not available from Third World countries or they are of poor quality. Collecting statistics is an advanced and expensive activity. Nevertheless, some statistics have been collected for the WHO.[3] [5] In addition, Professor Griffith Edwards of the Addiction Research Unit in London wrote to many psychiatrists around the world asking about alcohol problems in their countries. Some of the information he received along with a short review of published accounts has been published.[4]

Alcohol epidemiology is always difficult, but there are particular problems in Third World countries. Illicit production, for instance—which counts for little in most developed countries —is important. (The names of the "local brews" make hypnotic reading: *chang'aa* and *busaa* come from Kenya; *ogogoro* and *burukutu* from Nigeria; *chibuku, mbamba, solopi, mbote,* and *sikokiann* from Zambia; *guaro contrabando* from Costa Rica; *chicha, cocuy,* and *guaropo fuerte* from Venezuela; *aragi* and *marisa* from the Sudan; and *sur, lugri, chang, chami, rurba, soma, boja, zu, channa,* and *sugda* from India. Not surprisingly, the country with the toughest controls on alcohol has the richest vocabulary for illicit beverages.) A second problem is that the death rate from cirrhosis, which seems to be the best measure of alcohol-related problems in developed countries, is

a much poorer measure in Third World countries, where other causes of cirrhosis apart from alcohol are so much commoner. Then, as in the developed world, all figures that give a prevalence of "alcoholism" must be taken with a pinch of salt as widely divergent definitions of alcoholism are used. Finally, although figures on how much alcohol contributes to accidents are often quoted, few Third World countries have equipment to test routinely blood alcohol concentrations.

With all these provisos in mind I want to consider some of the information that is available; most of it is taken from information compiled for the WHO.[3] Firstly, however, world and continental production of alcohol is worth considering (table).[5] Between 1962 and 1972 recorded world production of

World and continental production of wine, beer, and spirit in 1960 and 1972

	Production in millions of litres	
	1960	1972
Wine		
World	24 251	28 897
Africa	2 268	1 604
Asia	72	173
South and Central America	2 421	3 042
Beer		
World	40 750	68 559
Africa	738	2 121
Asia	1 271	4 528
South and Central America	4 091	5 036
Spirit		
World	1 637	2 630
Africa	29	49
Asia	240	362
South and Central America	198	321

Source: WHO.[5]

wine increased by 19%, of spirits by 61%, and of beer by 68%. The production of beer increased by 187% in Africa, and that of spirits by 51% in Asia and by 62% in South America.

Figures on alcohol production and consumption tend always to be better than those for alcohol-related problems, but, as explained in the second chapter, the evidence that the two go closely together is good.[8]

AFRICA

Beer imports in Nigeria (a country that exports oil) increased from 1·3m l in 1970 to 132m l in 1976. No good figures were available on alcohol problems. Kenya is reported to have seen an increase in both alcohol consumption and admissions for alcoholism, but no exact statistics are available. The Kenya Brewery, however, increased its earnings by 33% from 1978 to 1979. In Zambia the production of alcohol has risen and fallen without any clearly discernible pattern; arrests for

Alcohol in the Third World

drunkenness more than quadrupled, however, between 1968 and 1973—from 3000 to 12 500. In Mauritius between 1972 and 1976 the production of rum was doubled and that of beer increased by 64%.

SOUTH AND CENTRAL AMERICA

Argentinians consume a great deal of wine, most of which they produce themselves, and in 1977 the mortality rate from cirrhosis was 18·1 per 100 000 (compared with about 4 in England and Wales and about 17 in France in the mid 1970s). About 10-15% of all general hospital admissions and 30% of all psychiatric admissions were for patients with alcohol-related problems.

Costa Rica increased its beer production from 9m l in 1961 to 48m l in 1976, and wine production trebled between 1977 and 1978, while spirit production increased by 9%. Illicit production is important in Costa Rica, and in one area there was one illicit still for every 2·7 houses. About 5% of the population of 2·05m were classified as "abnormal drinkers," and patients discharged from hospital with the diagnosis of alcoholism rose from 1874 in 1976 to 5135 in 1978. In 1977 20 577 of the 34 935 arrests for public disorder were for drunkenness.

Adult alcohol consumption per head in Mexico in 1972 was estimated to be 4·9 l of 100% alcohol, and two surveys found that about 12-18% of the population were "excessive drinkers." In 1974 the mortality from cirrhosis was 19·3 per 100 000. In 1977 some 51% of violent injuries were associated with alcohol, and absenteeism was estimated to cost $US 100m a year.

In Venezuela, another country that exports oil, beer production doubled between 1970 and 1976 and then increased by 21% in 1977. Spirit production rose by 536% between 1970 and 1976, while whisky imports rose from 0·3m l in 1945 to 13m l in 1976. Thus consumption per head almost doubled between 1961 and 1976. Alcohol was considered to be the main factor in half of all traffic accidents, and in 1978 traffic accidents were the commonest cause of death in Venezuela (sic). Crime and alcohol consumption are strongly associated in South and Central America, and a quarter to a half of all offences in Venezuela were committed under the influence of alcohol in 1974-6.

ASIA

In India the government is aiming at prohibiting alcohol totally and most of the population do not drink. "Country liquor" and beer production between them more than doubled between 1970 and 1977, however, and in some sections of the population alcohol is said to have replaced traditional drugs. In Sri Lanka consumption per head in men over 15 increased from 1·63 l 100% alcohol to 2·01 l in 1977, and one study found a prevalence of alcoholism of 28·7 per 1000 in men over 25.

THE CARIBBEAN

Alcohol abuse is a big problem in the West Indies. About 30 000 of the 1 100 000 people in Trinidad and Tobago were judged to be alcoholic in one study.

Why is there increased alcohol consumption and damage in the Third World?

Determining what makes societies, groups, and individuals drink as much as they do is very difficult. Hundreds of factors come into play, but certain of them may be tentatively teased out. We must remember also that the countries we conveniently describe as Third World differ greatly, and a factor that is important in one country may not be important in another.

54

Increasing wealth is undoubtedly important. Time and time again in developed countries the price of alcohol relative to average income has been found to be crucial in determining consumption. In a country such as Venezuela that has rapidly become richer this is probably very important. Erosion of old customs is probably also important, but, as Griffith Edwards has argued,[4] rapid social change and development do not lead automatically to increased alcohol problems. They do not seem to be the inevitable price of development, as some cynics have argued.

At opposite ends of the spectrum, high status and absolute poverty both seem to be associated with increased alcohol consumption in Third World countries. Those in the upper reaches of society not only have more money to spend on alcohol but they associate it with urbanity and sophistication. Meanwhile, in the slums of South and Central America (the *pavelas* in Brazil, the *ranchos* in Caracas, the *barriadas* in Lima, and the *villas miserias* in Argentina) people drink to forget and to enjoy themselves for at least an evening.

Finally, in a way that nobody seems to have been able to measure or describe, the alcohol producers of the developed world are promoting their products in Third World countries. They see markets open up and they try to sell their products as do all other manufacturers. Unfortunately they are selling problems at the same time.

Special problems for the developing world

Alcohol will cause problems in any society, and it will do so more as consumption rises, but Third World countries are in some ways specialy vulnerable.[4] Firstly, the tendency for the very poor and the privileged to be particularly affected has serious consequencies. For the very poor, who live on the edge of survival, an alcoholic father may mean death for members of the family. Furthermore, alcoholism and malnutrition are a particularly unhappy and dangerous combination. The society is likely to suffer badly if the professionals and the technocrats are removed through alcohol problems. Secondly, at all levels alcohol problems may interfere with national development as they are an important cause of lowered productivity, absenteeism, and accidents. Finally, patients with alcohol problems may put a large load on health services that are already likely to be overstretched.

What is being done and what can be done?

In a very few countries—such as India—the government is aiming at total prohibition of alcohol. In contrast, the governments in other countries—some African ones, for instance— do not see alcohol problems as important. Most countries, however, are paying some attention to the problems and are setting up agencies to look at alcohol. Some governments have banned alcohol advertising; many have introduced some kind of licensing system; many are instituting laws on alcohol and driving; some have work-based programmes; and a few have tried health education campaigns.[3] In most countries these "preventive" measures are also complemented by treatment and rehabilitation programmes.

WHO has suggested a blueprint for countries wishing to develop alcohol programmes.[5] It emphasises that a programme that includes prevention, treatment, and rehabilitation will be needed and that the programmes will need to fit into the overall framework of development. Some kind of co-ordinating body (preferably governmental) is recommended, and an alcohol policy should be formed. The WHO recommends the Ontario policy as an example. This has three main aims: maintaining the price of alcohol relative to disposable income; stopping any further relaxation of alcohol control measures; and educating the public on the social and individual danger of alcohol. Few countries, however, including most developed countries, have such a policy.

References

[1] Grant JP. *The state of the world's children 1981-82*. New York: UNICEF, 1981.

[2] Gilles HM. Malaria. *Br Med J* 1981;**283**:1382-5.

[3] Moser J, ed. *Prevention of alcohol-related problems. National and sub-national profiles of alcohol use, alcohol-related problems, and preventive measures, policies and programmes*. Geneva: WHO, 1980.

[4] Edwards G. Drinking problems: putting the Third World on the map. *Lancet* 1979;ii:402-4.

[5] Moser J, ed. *Prevention of alcohol-related problems. An international review of preventive measures, policies, and programmes*. Toronto: Alcoholism and Drug Addiction Research Foundation, 1980.

[6] Special Committee of the Royal College of Psychiatrists. *Alcohol and alcoholism*. London: Tavistock Publications, 1979.

[7] World Health Organisation Expert Committee. *Problems related to alcohol consumption*. Geneva: WHO, 1979.

[8] Davies DL, ed. *The Ledermann curve*. London: Alcohol Education Centre, 1977.

THE POLITICS OF ALCOHOL

In a saner world, where national sovereignty, military machismo, and governmental amour-propre counted for less, the politics of alcohol would probably be a great deal more important than the politics of the Falkland Islands. Disraeli said that: "The first priority of Government must be the health of the people," and yet the cabinet minister at the Department of Health and Social Security, despite being the biggest spender, is 18th in the pecking order. (He has recently been relegated.) About five times as many people as the entire population of the Falkland Islands die every year from alcohol in Britain, and many hundreds of thousands more suffer from the diverse effects of alcohol.[1] Not only life and happiness but that other essential of political dispute—money—is vitally important too: in 1979 Britons spent almost £9000m on alcohol (7·7% of all consumer expenditure); in 1980 the Government had an income of £3597m from tax on alcohol; in 1979 3·4% of the working population were employed in the drink industry; and in 1980 Britain had a positive balance of trade from alcohol of £449·3m.[2] Furthermore, there are many sides and factors in the potential conflict over alcohol. At one extreme are ardent prohibitionists, and at the opposite extreme bodies who insist on the rights of drink manufacturers and advertisers to market their products as aggressively as possible unhindered by any governmental intervention. In the middle are a host of governmental and non-governmental organisations and individuals concerned in some way with the many effects of alcohol.

The idea that some kind of political action is necessary to reduce alcohol damage is now well established. Professor R E Kendell made the case for political action very cogently in the BMJ in 1979,[3] and the World Health Organisation,[4] the Royal College of Psychiatrists,[1] and the Central Policy Review Staff (the Government "think tank")[5] have all taken a similar line. The decks are now being cleared for political action to combat alcohol problems, and this article looks at some of the many organisations who will have a part to play.

Need there be conflict?

Is it not journalism of the lowest and most sensational order to draw comparisons between the Falkland Islands crisis and the problems with alcohol abuse? Surely there are no "sides" in this issue, and every faction is concerned to reduce alcohol damage: drink manufacturers dislike drunkenness and cirrhosis of the liver just as much as doctors and other health and social workers do. A "negotiated settlement" would be much preferable to any kind of conflict between the drink trade and those concerned to reduce alcohol damage, but all the evidence is that this cannot be.

Alcohol damage in Britain—or, indeed, in any country—cannot be reduced without that country consuming less alcohol. The link between alcohol damage and consumption per head may not adhere exactly to the equation devised by Ledermann,[6] but all the evidence is that the relation is very close.[7] (See Chapter 2.) The shape of the curve that shows how many people drink how much cannot be changed, which means that if Britain consumes more then it will experience more alcohol damage. To reduce alcohol damage consumption must be reduced, and this conflicts *directly* with the interests of alcohol manufacturers. They will argue that by educating for moderation a country can drink more but have fewer people who drink a lot and experience damage. But the evidence suggests that this cannot happen, and so the drink industry and those concerned to reduce damage are thrown into conflict.

Therefore, should those who are concerned to reduce damage —researchers, educators, and treatment agencies—accept money from the drink industry because it has a lot to give and is only too anxious to be seen to be "doing good?" This is a question that each group is free to answer for itself, but any campaign that is effective in reducing consumption is unlikely to be offered any money anyway.

I want now to examine the various "sides" in the conflict. The drink industry is immense, rich, and powerful, whereas, as a recent report has pointed out, the anti-alcohol lobby is in complete disarray.[8] The Government, meanwhile, seems unwilling to take any clear line and leaves the different government departments concerned with alcohol to pull in different directions.

The drink trade

In 1979 in Britain there were: 81 brewing companies owning 142 breweries; 129 distilleries; 230 vineyards; 75 700 pubs and hotels selling drink; 20 000 private hotels and restaurants with restricted licences; 32 700 licensed and registered clubs; 41 100 off licences; and 12 000 independent wholesalers and importers.[2] Drink manufacturers have invested a lot of their large profits in new production and distribution facilities, and the industry is very modern and efficient; it does not suffer from the "British disease."[2] It is ready to expand greatly its production, although recently consumption has fallen off. About 750 000 people are employed in the drinks industry, and this is one of the few categories of employment that is expanding (table I). The jobs are dispersed all over the country, but some towns—for example, Burton-upon-Trent, Tadcaster, and Dufftown—are almost utterly dependent on the industry for jobs. Most of the beer, cider, and spirits drunk in Britain are manufactured by British companies in

TABLE I—*Changes in total number of employees, employees in manufacturing industry, and employees in the drink trade between 1970 and 1980 in UK*

Category	1970 (000)	1980 (000)	% change
All employees in employment	22 404	22 008	−1·8
All manufacturing industry	8 727	6 660	−23·7
All alcoholic drinks	600	750	+25·0

56

Britain. Furthermore, as I have said, alcohol brings in much needed foreign currency (table II) and revenue for the Government (table III).

TABLE II—*Imports and exports of alcoholic drinks in 1980*

Drink	Imports £m	Exports £m
Wine of fresh grape	284·5	24·6
Cider	0·6	3·3
Beer	35·6	19·0
(excluding Ireland)	(19·3)	(18·4)
Spirits	110·8	834·0
(of which whisky)	(6·2)	(747·6)
Total	431·6	880·9
(of which EEC)	(324·0)	(208·7)

TABLE III—*Revenue from alcoholic drinks in the fiscal year 1980*

Drink	Excise duty £m	VAT £m	Total £m
Beer	917	611	1528
Wine	362	218	580
Spirits	1152	325	1477
Cider	12	—	12
Total	2443	1154	3597
All tax receipts by HM Government			54331
(% Deriving from alcoholic drinks)			6·6

Many of the companies that produce alcohol are vast and have many other interests. The Imperial Group, for instance, has four divisions, including a tobacco division, which has the majority of the British market, and a brewing and leisure division.[9] The brewing division includes: the Courage Group and associated companies; John Smith's Tadcaster Brewery Ltd; and the Saccone and Speed Group, which owns many wine merchants—Arthur Cooper Ltd, for instance. Cantrell and Cochrane Ltd, Harp Lager Ltd, and Taunton Cider Co Ltd are associated companies. Table IV shows beers, lagers, and ciders produced by the group and wines and spirits supplied by them. In 1981 the group had sales of £4525·6m and profits before taxation of £106m: the trading surplus of the brewing division was £50·7m, a 20% increase on 1980.

TABLE IV—*Some of the brands of alcohol produced or distributed by the Imperial Group*

Ales and stouts
John Courage Strong Bitter; Courage Best Bitter; John Smith's Yorkshire Bitter; Tavern Ale; Courage AK; Directors' Bitter; Courage Midlands Mild; SIPA; Light Ale; Brown Ale; Velvet Stout; Bulldog Pale Ale; Magnet Pale Ale; Barley Wine; Imperial Russian Stout; Old Tom; John Smith's Export Pale; John Smith's Sweet Stout; John Smith's Double Brown; Magnet Old.

Malt liquor
Colt 45.

Lagers
Hofmeister (own brand); Harp; Kronenbourg; Henniger Diet Pils and Henniger Kaiser Pilsner (sole distribution rights in UK).

Cider
Taunton Cider.

Wines and spirits
Southern Comfort; Riccadonna Vermouth; Dry Cane White Rum; Lanson Champagne; Rocamar Spanish wine; Scotsmac; Glen Grant 8-year-old Scotch Malt Whisky; Hankey Bannister Scotch Whisky; Cherry Heering liqueur; Jack Daniels Tennessee whisky; Black Tower Liebfraumilch.

There are other companies of comparable size, and the five biggest breweries are among the 126 top companies in the UK.[10] The companies have trade organisations, which include the Brewers' Society, the Wine and Spirits Association, the Scotch Whisky Association, and the National Federation of Licensed Victuallers. When there was first talk of the anti-alcohol lobby forming a pressure group, the industry responded with the idea of forming a group specifically to oppose the new anti-alcohol organisation. With its huge economic power the industry

obviously has great political influence, and in 1979 it donated £107 445 to the Conservative Party and its associates.[11] Allied Breweries made the biggest donation of any company—£62 000.[11]

In addition, 35 members of Parliament have a direct financial interest in the drink trade and a further 39 have an indirect interest.[12 13] Ministers are required to give up their outside connections, but, before becoming a minister, Norman Fowler, the present Secretary of State at the DHSS, was a director of a subsidiary company of J Walter Thompson, one of the world's leading advertising agencies, which has large alcohol accounts, and Geoffrey Finsburg, a junior minister at the DHSS, was a parliamentary adviser to the National Union of Licensed Victuallers.

Other groups have a heavy interest in Britons continuing to drink as much as they do. Foremost among these are advertising companies: £100m is spent each year on advertising and promoting alcohol, making it one of the largest sources of revenue to advertisers.[14] The Advertising Association has a team working all the time gathering evidence to try to show that an advertising ban would do nothing to reduce alcohol damage.[15] Through advertising the media, too, benefit greatly from alcohol revenue, and this applies even to the BBC, who often televise events sponsored by alcohol producers.

The anti-alcohol lobby

The power, influence, wealth, efficiency, and modernity of the drink trade contrast greatly with the sad disarray of the anti-alcohol lobby. A DHSS study group appointed by Sir George Young when he was a minister at the DHSS to look into the effectiveness of the voluntary organisations concerned with reducing alcohol damage reported two weeks ago and found "serious deficiencies."[8] These findings came as no surprise to those familiar with the organisations.

The report was written by John James and Jan Filochowski from the DHSS from the Policy Strategy Unit, and Nicholas Hinton and Francis Gladstone from the National Council for Voluntary Organisations. They looked at no fewer than seven anti-alcohol organisations which receive funds from the DHSS: the National Council on Alcoholism; the Medical Council on Alcoholism; the Alcohol Education Centre; the Federation of Alcoholic Rehabilitation Establishments; Turning Point; Alcoholism Community Centres for Education, Prevention, and Treatment; and Alcoholic Recovery Project. The study group concentrated on the first four of these organisations, which between them received £300 000 from the DHSS in 1980-1. All four, but particularly the National Council on Alcoholism and the Medical Council on Alcoholism, were strongly criticised in the report, which recommended that they should be scrapped and a new organisation created.

The report suggested that there were five main tasks for those concerned to reduce alcohol damage: public education and prevention, including influencing Government; co-ordinating services for problem drinkers, including work-based programmes; training both primary workers and specialists; advising and supporting local services; and providing a forum for debate. The group identified these five main tasks for two reasons. Firstly, because duplication of work and rivalry are two of the main problems with the existing organisations, and in a brighter future the tasks should be clearly defined and allocated to particular organisations. Secondly, the group suggests that drink trade money will be acceptable for financing some of these tasks—treatment, training, and research, for instance—but not others, particularly political preventive campaigns.

The report recommended that the new national voluntary organisation would: inform and advise local services; plan and develop services and training; make grants for training; and work with industry. The Health Education Council (and presumably the Scottish Health Education Group, although the report does not specifically mention it, as the DHSS remit does not cover Scotland), meanwhile, should expand its programme

The politics of alcohol

on alcohol problems. The medical royal colleges should take over part of the Medical Council on Alcoholism's role and promote the study of alcohol problems in undergraduate and postgraduate medical education. Finally, the job of political campaigning, the report recommends, should be taken on by a "small and compact organisation," which would start under the aegis of the medical royal colleges and later be sponsored by the DHSS.

The group knew when writing its report that such an organisation was waiting in the wings. The presidents of the royal colleges have been discussing the project for over a year, and there is every hope that it might begin before the end of 1982. It will be modelled on the successful Action on Smoking and Health (ASH), but will have an even more formidable job to do in changing public attitudes and countering the might of the drink trade.

Kenneth Clarke, the Minister of Health, has called for reactions to the report by the end of June. The workers of the various organisations criticised will naturally be upset, but most people interested in and working with alcohol problems will probably agree with the conclusions of the report and look forward to a long overdue reorganisation.

The Government: "piggy in the middle"

Poised between the might of the drink trade and the ineffectiveness of the present anti-alcohol lobby is the Government, which is pulled in many different directions. Sixteen different Government departments have some interest in alcohol; table V shows the departments and their interests. The Treasury, the most powerful Government department, is concerned that the enormous revenue that it gets from alcohol should not be threatened by a greatly reduced consumption. The Department of Trade wants to please the drink industry, while the Department of Employment will want to ensure that jobs provided by the trade are kept intact. The DHSS, however, should be aiming at reducing alcohol consumption. Over and above this, the politicians will not want to do anything to upset the electorate, which, as a *Sunday Times* poll showed, is not yet ready to accept any drastic political action to cut consumption.[16]

So with so many departments concerned with alcohol, many of them pulling in different directions, should there be a department or an interdepartmental committee concerned exclusively with alcohol, which could co-ordinate Government policy? The Central Review Staff considered this question and decided that there should be: it recommended the formation of an Advisory Council on Alcohol Problems. In considering the question it pointed out that according to the WHO Britain was exceptional in not having a co-ordinating agency, and it concluded that: "Neither the existing machinery within Government nor the bodies outside it provide the means for coherent formulation of policies. . . ."

The Government, however, has ignored this sound advice, which was offered in 1979. The Government wants to "have its cake and eat it," and to have ample scope for carrying out contradictory policies suits it well. Significantly the Central Policy Review Staff report, agreed to be a sensible, clear, and progressive report,[17] was never published. What has been published is *Drinking Sensibly*,[18] an inept and uninteresting booklet that seems mostly to be concerned with providing excuses for Government inaction. The alcohol equivalent of ASH is badly needed.

TABLE V—*Government departments concerned with alcohol*

Department of Health and Social Security

Trends in the effects of alcohol consumption. Health and social service provision for victims of alcohol misuse. Health education on alcohol. Sponsoring research into alcohol abuse and related problems.

Ministry of Agriculture, Fisheries, and Food

Sponsorship of alcohol industry, including distribution and retailing. International aspects, trade, that bear on the wellbeing of industry. Regulation of drinks for purity, *etc.* Nutritional aspects of alcohol consumption.

Home Office

Licensing law. Offences of drunkenness. Other criminal offences associated with consumption of alcohol and treatment of offenders with alcohol problems. Police interest in drink related road accidents. Broadcast advertising of alcoholic drinks, in the context of the Home Office sponsorship responsibilities for broadcasting.

Law Commission Office

Function of JPs in licensing laws.

Department of Transport

Road accidents and related legislation (Great Britain, in association with Scottish Office).

Department of the Environment

Football hooliganism, as affected by alcohol (with Home Office). Sponsorship of sport by alcohol industry.

Customs and Excise

Duties on alcoholic drink, including international negotiations.

Treasury

Fiscal policy. Prices. Balance of payments for trade in alcohol. Economic significance of alcohol industry. Public expenditure effects of alcohol abuse.

Department of Trade

Prices. Competition and pricing policy as it bears on the alcohol industry, including distribution and retailing. Policy on container sizes and metrication. Consumers' interest in advertising and promotion. International trade in alcoholic drinks. Press and cinema film industries. Alcohol consumption in the Merchant Navy and the civil aviation industry. Tourism.

Department of Employment

Effect of alcohol abuse on accidents, absenteeism, and productivity.

Department of Education and Science

Health education in schools. Effect of alcohol on young people in education.

Civil Service Department

Effect of alcohol abuse on the efficiency and conduct of the civil service.

Ministry of Defence

Policies affecting the control of alcohol in the armed Services and the treatment of its misuse.

Scottish Office
Welsh Office
Northern Ireland Departments

Conclusions on political action

Political initiatives to limit alcohol damage would include actions such as: regular increases in the tax on alcohol at least to maintain its real price; a ban on alcohol advertising; reduction in the number of alcohol outlets; stiffer laws on drunken driving, including random breathalysing; a ban on any further loosening of the licensing laws; and an increase in the educational campaigning on the problems of alcohol. Just as with action on smoking what is really needed is a Government committed to reducing the harm and which acts in a co-ordinated way to achieve that end. But political action will be neither easy nor a panacea. There is formidable opposition to any political measures designed to cut consumption. Furthermore, as Poland shows, political action in isolation may not always have the desired effect, and to reduce alcohol damage action must continue on every front, including education and treatment.

Many people have helped me in writing these articles, and I thank all of them. Particularly I thank Marcus Grant, Dr Martin Plant, Mike Daube, Dr David Player, Dr Norman Kreitman, Professor R E Kendall, Dr Bruce Ritson, Dr John Saunders, Freddie Lawrence, Adrian Pollitt, Professor Griffith Edwards, Joy Moser, Dr Hilary Clough, Olwen Glynn Owen, Professsor Sir Desmond Pond, Sir George Young, M J Waterson, Chris Thurman, Dr Shirley Otto, Bill Saunders, and Derek Rutherford. None of these people are likely, however, to agree with everything that I have written.

All the information in the chapter on Poland has come to me from Professor I Wald, Jacek Moskalewicz, and Antoni Bielewicz—all of the Psychoneurological Institute, Warsaw. I am very grateful for all the help and kindness they showed me.

The photograph in the chapter on the habitual drunken offender was kindly supplied by Consortium.

References

[1] Special Committee of the Royal College of Psychiatrists. *Alcohol and alcoholism.* London: Tavistock Publications, 1979.
[2] Thurman CW. The structure and role of the alcoholic drinks industry. In: Grant M, Plant M, Williams A, eds. *Economics and alcohol:*